WHO YOU ARE IS HOW YOU PARENT

A MODERN MONK'S GUIDE TO
PARENTING YOUR STRUGGLING TEEN

Who You Are Is How You Parent

JIVAN DAS

HOUNDSTOOTH
PRESS

COPYRIGHT © 2026 JIVAN DAS
All rights reserved.

WHO YOU ARE IS HOW YOU PARENT
A Modern Monk's Guide to Parenting Your Struggling Teen

FIRST EDITION

ISBN 978-1-5445-5135-7 *Hardcover*
       978-1-5445-5134-0 *Paperback*
       978-1-5445-5136-4 *Ebook*

To Maa, who gives me everything.

Contents

INTRODUCTION...9

PART 1: UNDERSTANDING THEM
1. WHY TEENS STRUGGLE..21
2. CAN'T VS. WON'T..31
3. HOW TO HELP WITHOUT HELPING..39
4. EVERYTHING SERVES..47
5. THE TRUST TIGHTROPE 55
6. THE SOUND OF SILENCE 63

PART 2: UNDERSTANDING US
7. IS IT ME, OR IS IT THEM?..79
8. WHAT DRIVES OUR STRUGGLES 89
9. RESCUING AND PROBLEM-SOLVING...97
10. WHAT ABOUT OUR TRIGGERS?...111

PART 3: FUNDAMENTALS OF STRUCTURE
11. STRUCTURAL LEVERAGE... 133
12. SAYING YES AND NO 149
13. THE ART OF SETTING BOUNDARIES...161

PART 4: FUNDAMENTALS OF COMMUNICATION
14. HOW TO SPEAK SO THEY LISTEN 183
15. HOW TO LISTEN SO THEY SPEAK 189
16. THE HARD CONVERSATION 195

CONCLUSION...205
RESOURCES... 209

Introduction

I've got a question for you. Do you love your kid enough to question everything you were taught about parenting, everything you know about your kid, and everything you think you know about yourself? If so, you are ready to read this book.

Picking up this book means there is a good chance you're watching someone you love struggle, and you're feeling helpless. So many of the choices they make seem designed to push you away and make their life harder. You've tried everything, and the gap between you both seems to get wider every day. This book won't save them from their pain, but it will help you learn how to show up for it and be with them in ways that actually make a difference.

THE REAL WORK OF PARENTING

Parenting isn't just about guiding your kids. It's about how you grow as you guide. Your willingness to lead creates your own transformation, and this book will accelerate that growth in ways that will surprise you.

You'll learn insightful strategies that make perfect sense. Situations that felt impossible will become clearer and more manageable. Your relationship with your kid will get stronger, even in the midst of their struggle. And most importantly, you'll understand how their pain is teaching you both something essential.

Here's something I really want you to know: You don't have to be perfect. You just have to be willing to look inside yourself and show up differently—especially when things get hard. Here's what that will look like.

WHAT YOU'LL DISCOVER

This book will reveal *why* your kid struggles—regardless of what form that struggle takes. You'll learn strategies for creating real influence that you've probably never encountered before. And you'll understand the unintentional and unconscious mistakes you're making right now, along with how to avoid them.

The foundation of everything in these pages rests on one principle: **Understanding is the gateway to transformation.** When you comprehend the deeper forces driving your kid's behavior, everything shifts. You'll move from reacting to their symptoms to responding to their real needs, from feeling confused and helpless to being clear and purposeful in your response.

After reading this book, you'll have a renewed sense of confidence and optimism born from a deeper understanding of both your kid's struggles and your own. But before we dive into strategies and solutions, I want you to know who's guiding you on this journey.

I WAS YOUR KID

I was a version of your kid. I was angry. I was sad. I was depressed. I stole. I lied. I hated my parents, and I hated myself. I got high (a lot), drank booze (a lot), and pushed away anyone who tried to understand me. I got bullied, and I bullied others because I hated how I felt inside.

From the outside, my high school years looked fantastic—I had lots of friends, got good grades, went to parties, played sports, and was friends with all the popular kids. But underneath that thin veneer lived profound insecurity. I masked it by doing anything to fit in: smoking weed, getting drunk, being reckless, using self-deprecating humor for attention. I distanced myself from people who could see something was wrong. I did anything I could think of to escape the confusing turmoil inside.

I hated my parents because they represented control. Their love felt repulsive because I hated myself. I couldn't stand how I looked—I was short, I had big ears and big teeth, and I hit puberty later than everyone else my age. I felt totally worthless inside. And that pain became my purpose.

FROM STRUGGLE TO SERVICE

Struggle became a great guide, however. I've dedicated my entire twenty-five year career to working with young people and families who struggle like I did. I've spent more than seventy-five thousand clinical hours working with thousands of teens and families in crisis. I am a licensed psychotherapist with a master's degree in Counseling Psychology, and I have devoted myself to becoming the clinical therapist, teacher, and disarming guy my clients need.

I know what it takes for young people and families to

move from crisis to thriving. I've seen them do it again and again. And this book will teach you to do the same.

In addition to clinical expertise and sophistication, this book is based on all I've learned on my personal path of transformation. In fact, I've devoted my life to transformation. I started practicing meditation and (reluctantly) engaging in my own personal therapy in 2001. Over the next fifteen years, I grew to actually love transformational work. I attended dozens of personal development workshops as a participant before becoming trained in leading these kinds of workshops. I have taught thousands of people how to experience real transformation like I did. In short, I love growing and helping other people grow.

Then I became a celibate monk.

The spiritual path provided a level of fulfillment I had been looking for my entire life. I love meditation and practice it two hours a day. I've logged over fifteen thousand hours of meditation over the last twenty years. I follow a vegetarian diet, abstain from drugs and alcohol, and—most importantly—have the great privilege to devote all that I am to the upliftment of other people.

AN OFFERING

This unique combination of lived experience, clinical expertise, and practical transformational tools shapes everything you'll read in these pages. This book is an expression of devotion—to you. These pages are the sum of who I am—a former struggling youth turned clinician, teacher, and monk, with all my strengths and weaknesses.

This book distills this knowledge into clear, practical terms that will transform your relationship with your kid who struggles in ways you may not have considered. No psychological jargon or theoretical platitudes—just strategies and principles that work.

THE JOURNEY STARTS NOW

Reading this book is a journey, and we'll begin where you are now: confused, worried, and feeling like nothing works. By the end, you'll better understand not just your kid, but also yourself. You'll have practical tools that make a difference. Most importantly, you'll discover that your teen's struggle isn't a problem to solve; it's an invitation to become the parent they need and the person you were always meant to be.

The path ahead isn't easy, but it's worth it. You'll be asked to see things differently, to look honestly at yourself, to let go of what isn't working and embrace what does. There will be moments of recognition that sting, insights that challenge what you know about parenting, and breakthroughs that change how you see both your kid and yourself.

And here's a promise: If you're willing to do this work, if you're ready to understand before trying to be understood, if you can stay curious instead of certain, you'll discover something profound. Your kid's struggle—the very thing that brought you to this book—might just be the doorway to the deepest, most authentic relationship you've ever had with them.

Let's begin with a simple but critical shift: Instead of asking "How do I help?" you'll ask "How do I understand?" Because understanding, as you're about to discover, is where everything begins.

PART 1

Understanding Them

> **There's something your kid craves more than freedom and more than being left alone—and most parents never offer it.**
>
> They need you to see them. When you better understand their struggles, you'll experience a shift in how you relate to them. Without grasping the nature of their challenges, you're trying to unlock a door with the wrong key. Understanding requires patience, humility, and a willingness to see someone's life experience from a totally new perspective.

MY WILD YEARS

First, a story: As a teenager, I was the one who got attention by telling crass jokes and doing wild shit other kids wouldn't do, like smashing car windows, destroying basketball hoops, and stealing beer from garages and grocery stores. On weekends I snuck out, got drunk, and drove my friends through the late, quiet nights of Green Bay, Wisconsin. We got high, shotgunned beers in my car, played video games, and threw bonfire parties in the woods until dawn. When I couldn't find weed, I was forced to face the depression created by my terribly low self-esteem that I was trying so desperately to avoid.

CRUSHED OPEN

There was one moment though, when someone got through—and it was unforgettable.

Each year, I played tennis in high school because it was the one sport I could find where size and strength didn't quite matter. In the months before varsity tryouts, I practiced more than I had for anything else. I hit the ball against a brick wall in oppressive summer heat and played matches nearly every day with my friends and teammates. For the first time in my life, I worked hard at something.

When the final tryouts came, my partner and I played doubles against two teammates who were pure athletes. They were strong, handsome, talented young men. We were scrawny boys. They hadn't practiced. They played tennis as a hobby and easily excelled at the other sports they liked more. Even though my partner and I were nervous, we felt well prepared and were confident that our practice had paid off. However, very early in the match, it became clear that our opponents' athleticism, power, and natural abilities far surpassed our meager physicality and insufficient training.

We got crushed in quick fashion.

THE MELTDOWN

As match point came and went, reality set in. We sucked. I sucked. I had made achieving this one thing my primary goal and failed. Miserably. It was a perfect manifestation of how I thought about myself: *Try as hard as you want; you'll always be something you wish you weren't.* In this case, a failure.

As the match ended, the other team and my partner approached the net to shake hands. I abruptly turned and walked off the court away from them.

"Hey, what are you doing?" my coach asked.

Fury erupted in me. Before I could think, I hucked my racket into the air with a loud "FUUUUUCK!!!"

A pregnant silence emerged in the large indoor tennis complex as my voice and clanging racket echoed across the sweeping ceiling and walls. My coach was infuriated. "J, what's wrong with you?"

I ignored him and walked stoically to my car amid the deafening stillness and shocked gazes of the people I practiced with for years. I drove home sullen and silent.

When my parents asked about tryouts, I snubbed them and stormed up to my room. I hated my jock friends who so easily dispatched with our best efforts, and I hated myself for being such a loser. My mom knocked on my bedroom door, asking if I was okay. I ignored her. It reminded me of how I hated her and my dad for reasons I couldn't articulate.

I sat alone in my room for an hour as the dark, cold Midwestern winter encroached on the cloudy afternoon. Slowly, I realized how awful I felt. Anger bled into shame. I hated being me. All of my attempts at being good at something, at anything, revealed one inexorable truth: *I sucked*.

TWO WORDS THAT CHANGED EVERYTHING

Over that hour, something began to emerge from the despair: regret. I didn't like how I had lost my shit after the match. I felt bad for disrespecting the tennis community, and especially my coach. So, I mustered the confidence to call him. As his phone rang, I welled up with emotion. I considered hanging up, smoking weed, playing video games, and going to bed—like I had so many times before. But I didn't.

When he answered, I hesitated. Then I said, "Hey, it's me."

No other words came out. There was just corked, raw emotion that had been fermenting for years. Silence. I did what I could to choke back tears.

My coach interrupted the long silence with two simple words that I'll never forget: "It's okay."

I couldn't hold it in anymore—sadness, shame, and self-hatred spilled out of me in cathartic, sobbing waves. I attempted to stumble through explanations about how hard

I practiced and what it meant to win, but I only got out a word or two between breathless, coughing tears.

He repeated, "It's okay... It's okay."

Eventually, I squeaked out an apology. "I'm just really sorry."

He said, "I know. It's okay."

THE POWER OF UNDERSTANDING

Understanding informs. Somehow my coach *understood* what my anger was about. He showed up in a way that softened my defenses and allowed me to express my pain. He gave me a gift I didn't know I needed: *permission to be broken.*

This is what your kid who is struggling needs from you—not solutions, not lectures, not even help as you know it. They need to be seen and understood, even in their messiness, their anger, and their apparent self-destruction.

The challenge is that you can't give what you don't have. You can't understand someone else's pain if you're running from your own. You can't create a warm welcome for their vulnerability if you're armored against your own.

So let's start this journey together with a critical shift: *from trying to fix to learning to understand.* This isn't about becoming passive or permissive. It's about becoming present—so *here*, so *available* that your kid feels safe enough to let you into their tender places where healing happens.

We'll begin our focus with understanding their struggles, their protective mechanisms, and their desperate need for connection disguised as rejection. Because once you can see past their behavior to their heart, so much becomes possible.

CHAPTER 1

Why Teens Struggle

"You had no right to do that! I don't want anything to do with it!"

Months before the deadline, James is the one who brings up an elite summer coding boot camp. He researched it himself, showed it to his parents, and told them it is exactly where he wants to spend his summer. They are thrilled. They agree immediately to cover the cost, and the plan is simple: James will handle the application; they will handle the bill.

But the weeks go by and nothing happens. Gentle reminders are met with "I'm working on it." The deadline creeps closer. Not wanting him to lose the opportunity he's been so excited about, his parents step in and submit the application themselves.

When he finds out, he completely falls apart.

His parents are blindsided. *What the hell is happening here? We spent months tracking this down and pulling strings to*

> *get him in—and he's acting like we insulted him? Have we raised an ungrateful brat?*

Here's the deal: James isn't the problem. Neither are his parents. The real issue is that no one understands what's actually going on beneath the surface.

So before we jump to quick fixes or blame games, we need to slow down and ask: What's really going on here? What's driving his reaction? What's the actual struggle about?

Real solutions don't come from rushing to judgment. They emerge naturally when we first invest in genuine understanding. It's like gardening—you can't force flowers to bloom, but when you tend the soil with patience and care, they blossom on their own.

The same is true for people. Hearts open when people feel seen and understood, not when they're being fixed or managed. This is the transformative power of understanding. So let's dive deeper into James's story to see what that understanding actually looks like.

THE PAIN BEHIND THE OUTBURST

When young people respond in seemingly insane ways to normal situations, there's always pain driving their reaction. Pain has a sneaky way of creating a protective story. People believe and express that story rather than feel the vulnerable (and terrifying) truth of what they're actually experiencing.

James has been quietly unraveling for months. Despite his sharp mind, he's been falling further behind in school, increasingly convinced he isn't as capable as everyone around him believes. He keeps up appearances—cracking jokes, projecting confidence, looking fine—but underneath, he's drowning in shame and exhausted by the effort of faking it.

When James loses his temper, his parents do their best to set aside their shock and listen to his perspective. But the conversation never gets deeper than his rage about the program they've signed him up for.

The parents are exhausted and came to me for help. I guide them to not fall into the trap of reacting to his response. And I remind them: When you soften, your kid softens. When you react, your kid reacts. When you judge, he *defends*. His reaction is based on a profoundly painful wound whose defense inspires a spoiled response.

In moments like these, ally with the part of your kids that's fighting to say and do the right thing, the part that wants to be open—the part that wants to be the good person they have forgotten they are. They likely feel lost, hopeless, and silenced by the pain in their world.

Struggle can bring out the worst in people. Your job as a caregiver during spikes of suffering is to be the calm, emotionally reliable, attuned person your kid needs. The more consistently you embody this, the more young people will create that calm for themselves from within.

Was James's response wildly self-absorbed? Absolutely. Is that all that's going on within him? Definitely not.

THE REAL STORY

Every struggle is an expression of an external challenge, an internal challenge, or both. James is only this way when he's overwhelmed, stressed, or holding something in that he needs to let out. He has the ability to be kind, grateful, humble, and hardworking. So, what's the deal?

He's actually a bright, perceptive kid with genuine potential. But for the past year, a creeping inner narrative has been running the show: *You're not as smart as they think you are. Eventually, everyone is going to find out.* He's convinced that the version of himself his parents and teachers believe in is a fiction he can barely maintain. Rather than risk exposing that fiction by asking for help, he white-knuckles it through each day in silence—appearing fine while slowly falling apart inside.

James can't accept the more accurate perspective that his parents and I share with him: "Everyone struggles. Needing support isn't weakness—it's how people actually grow. The fact that you've been working this hard just to hold it together says more about your character than any grade ever could. You have real gifts. Let people help you express them."

He stays in his comfort zone of silent suffering rather than taking the micro-risks of vulnerability that might contradict the painful inner narrative. He's waiting to feel capable and confident before he takes action. Unfortunately, confidence comes from working through discomfort—from taking risks, failing, and eventually succeeding. His silence keeps him stuck in a loop of familiar shame.

THE HIDDEN EMBARRASSMENT

So in order to really understand what's going on with your kid, **look at what's really happening emotionally.** In James's case, we discovered that months earlier he had confidently told his closest friends—and a teacher he deeply admired—that he was planning to apply to the boot camp on his own. He made it clear he didn't want anyone's help and that he'd get in based on his own ability.

He never applied.

When his parents surprised him with an enrollment they had quietly arranged on his behalf, he was humiliated—not because of the program itself, but because now his friends and that teacher would find out. They'd know he hadn't done it himself. They'd know he'd been bluffing. And in his mind, this confirmed everything he feared: He was a fraud, and now everyone would see it.

Of course, the reality was far simpler. His friends wouldn't think twice about who turned in the application. And his teacher would only be proud he was going at all. But this is the power of a narrative created and reinforced in shame—the distortions it produces feel more real than reality itself.

If his friends see him as someone capable and driven, then he actually *is* capable and driven. But if they find out his parents "arranged it all," he'll be exposed as the helpless pretender he's always feared he is. His terror of being found out is really just a reflection of how mercilessly he judges himself.

When James's parents initially focused on his meltdown over their generous gift, they missed what was really happening. They saw an entitled, ungrateful kid throwing a tantrum—and had no idea his entire sense of self was on the line.

Fortunately, I was able to coach James to share his hidden fears with his parents, and they completely understood the position he had put himself in. It was a beautiful healing moment for everyone and a profound lesson for his parents: **Look beneath the surface; be slow to judge and eager to understand.**

This kind of misunderstanding is the biggest way parents accidentally fuel their kids' struggles. So let's look more deeply at the nature of suffering itself so you can even more deeply understand why your kid is struggling.

WHY PEOPLE SUFFER

Why do people suffer? Underneath all the drama and chaos, there are layers of invisible interpretations, meanings, and hidden false beliefs driving everything for these people. The nature of suffering is complex, but its anatomy is surprisingly simple: It comes from (1) *the past* and (2) *beliefs*. That's it.

It takes courage to confront oneself and the beliefs one carries. And courage requires vulnerability. It means taking the risk of people being in more pain than they already are. But the problem is people who are already drowning in suffering aren't exactly lining up to take more risks. They don't have the emotional reserves to push themselves into even scarier territory.

When people don't challenge their limiting beliefs—like *I'm not worthy of love, I'm a failure, I'll never be good at anything*, or even *I'm perfect and have no flaws*—their lives get worse. Why? Because every choice we make is secretly informed by these unconscious limiting beliefs about ourselves and the world.

Even though a teenager's life might feel like absolute hell, it still has two immutably compelling qualities: *familiarity and predictability*. Which means they feel safe. Kids will choose the misery they know over the terrifying risk of being vulnerable and potentially getting hurt even worse.

Take the case of an amazing young woman who keeps making self-destructive choices. She's incredibly talented and has a wonderful personality, but she refuses to see it. She is becoming more fake, dressing in provocative ways that aren't really her, and starting to sneak out at night and skip school. So why is she acting this way, and why is it so hard for her to change?

If she acknowledged her strengths, was more authentic, and started following rules again, she'd have to face two brutal realities: (1) how much she's betraying herself through her current decisions, and (2) all the temporary discomfort that comes with being truly vulnerable. If she "opens up" about what she is struggling with, she has to feel everything she's been running from—and that is completely overwhelming. Recognizing her actual potential would shatter the identity of self-loathing she's built her world around.

Looking within is terrifying for kids. And that's exactly why they fight it so hard.

THE SELF-ESTEEM CONNECTION

Every kid who struggles has a self-esteem issue—even the ones who seem overly confident. In those cases, the kids who brag the most about their greatness are usually running the furthest and the fastest from their own self-doubt and insecurity.

When kids have been spiraling for months—or crash and burn overnight—the overwhelm hits especially hard. It can destroy any chance of getting back up. The overwhelm shows up as soul-crushing shame, humiliation, or vicious inner voices that never stop. These amazing kids end up sabotaging every relationship with anyone who can see past their armor into the scared, broken person hiding inside.

What makes it even more painful is deep down, they know their actions go against what they actually believe in. So when they're forced to look at the mess they've created, they're not just facing their mistakes—they're facing the part of themselves that hates who they've become.

It's like living with a mirror that only reflects your worst moments—magnified and distorted. No wonder they turn away. This creates a devastating cycle that's hard to see from the outside and feels inescapable from the inside.

THE BETRAYAL

Let's use metaphor to more accurately understand the predicament of the young person who struggles: Imagine you're in a post-apocalyptic wasteland. Your family is starving, and you're all going to die unless you can find food, water, and shelter. There's only one way to get what you need: betray your best friend whom you've shared your entire life with. Maybe you steal from them, lie to them, or hurt them in order to survive. They may never notice what you've done—and if they did, they would likely forgive you because they would know you did it to survive.

The brutal part here? Your kid is both people in this scenario.

They're the one doing the betraying, and they're also the friend being betrayed. The "food, water, and shelter" they're desperately chasing is their social status, their image, and their fleeting moments of feeling okay about themselves.

And the friend they keep betraying? That's their authentic self: their value, their integrity, and their innate self-love.

They're convinced betraying themselves doesn't matter because they're already so numb to their own pain. In their mind, there's no consequence to feeling worse when they already feel like garbage. They couldn't possibly feel more worthless, so why bother trying to feel better?

WHEN SURVIVAL LOOKS LIKE SELFISHNESS

I know this is heavy stuff. It's good to acknowledge your own feelings in this moment—and remember, the more you understand your kid, the more you can help. Let yourself feel whatever is coming up, and let's continue to understand the anatomy of their suffering.

Most parents describe their kids who struggle as wildly

self-absorbed. That makes sense, because *their suffering creates selfishness*. A drowning person will drown others who are trying to save them. Your child isn't selfish; they're drowning.

Think about this: When you stub your toe or smash your finger, do you immediately worry about someone else's feelings? Of course not. You're consumed by your own pain. Yet somehow we expect teenagers who are emotionally dying inside to immediately consider how their actions affect everyone and everything around them.

I'm not saying we should abandon expectations for kids who struggle, or even give them a free pass to hurt others just because they're suffering. Absolutely not. We just need to take a minute to keenly evaluate what we're demanding from someone who's barely surviving.

Most importantly, we need to understand that when they seem selfish, they're just trying to stay alive. Once we get this—that their struggle is survival, not defiance—everything about our approach can shift.

THE FIRST BREAKTHROUGH

In our earlier example with James, he wasn't broken—he was just really stressed—and your kid isn't broken, either. What looks like defiance, entitlement, or self-destruction is just a sophisticated protective system doing exactly what it was designed to do: keep them safe from more pain.

After understanding this, a lot of parents want to rush in and help, but they get met with even more resistance. Why? Because there's a crucial distinction a lot of parents miss—one that determines whether your attempts to help actually help, or whether they make things worse.

CHAPTER 2

Can't vs. Won't

"Sweetie, it's time to get up," a mother announces from the bathroom down the hall. "Remember, we talked about this. You have to go today."

"I can't!" her daughter says pleadingly, burying her face in her pillow. "I told you, there's no way I can go."

Meet Sarah, who bristles at the idea of going to high school almost every day. Her anxiety didn't show up overnight, though. It started as a quiet undercurrent in childhood—worries, fears, needing extra reassurance. By middle school, she began avoiding group activities, stopped seeing friends, and gradually pulled away from social situations. Now, the anxiety feels like quicksand—the harder she struggles against it, the deeper she sinks. When Sarah does make it to school, the pressure is overwhelming. Panic attacks, tears, and shutting down are common weekly occurrences.

She says she *can't*. And the question for her parents immediately becomes: *Does she really mean she can't? Or is it that she won't?*

THE REAL QUESTION

That's not just semantics. It's actually one of the most important distinctions we can make when figuring out how to support a kid who's struggling. When they're falling apart, are they *unable* or *unwilling* to handle what they're dealing with? This distinction between ability and desire is crucial because it fundamentally changes how you respond as a parent. Here's how to tell the difference and what to do about each one.

If it's lack of desire (won't): You can explore what's behind the resistance. Resistance is protection. Refusing to do something usually means they're refusing to face some aspect of themselves. Sometimes it's simple—homework is boring, teachers suck. These refusals are easily handled with clear expectations: "If you don't do your homework, you can't go out."

But sometimes it's more complex. "What don't you like about your teachers?"

"They suck at teaching."

Translation: "I don't understand the subject, and they're not helping me learn." This kid thinks she's stupid (and she thinks other people do, too) and won't engage because it means navigating this inner criticism.

If it's lack of ability (can't): Treating it like willfulness is like yelling at someone with broken legs to just walk already. Picture this exchange:

"You need to do your homework."

"I don't want to."

"If you don't, then you can't go out."

What they might not be saying is *"But I don't know how"*—because that's vulnerable, it shows "weakness," and they already feel insecure about not being good enough in school.

The challenge is that "can't" and "won't" often look identical from the outside. A kid's explosive "I won't do it!" might actually be their way of saying "I can't handle this"—but they'd rather appear defiant and powerful than admit they feel weak and vulnerable.

THE HIDDEN TRUTH BEHIND DEFIANCE

When young people get defiant, their "I won't do it" is usually a deeply believed but ultimately false "I *can't* do it." If we only see their refusal as pure stubbornness, we miss something critical: Defiance masks insecurity.

Take Jake, a high school kid whose world just imploded. His girlfriend cheated on him. His friends started hanging out with different people, and they stopped inviting him to their parties. One morning when his mom wakes him at the usual six-thirty, he declares, "I'm not going to school today. Don't try to convince me—I won't do it. I'll just skip class if you make me go."

For Jake, this "won't" is absolutely a "can't"—at least in his mind. He feels completely unable to face the pressures waiting for him: awkward conversations, figuring out where to sit at lunch, and dealing with teachers who seem to hate him.

His parents give him a pass for the day but tell him he has to go back tomorrow. The next morning? Same scene, different day. This time, they hold firm and try to make him go to school.

He refuses. An argument erupts. He screams about how much he fucking hates them and his life. Then he slams his door so hard the house shakes.

His parents stand there stunned, confused, and terrified. *What do we do? How did we get here?* To understand what just happened, we need to look at the deeper pattern.

THE GREAT ESCAPE

For kids who struggle, it's way easier to refuse to do something than to admit they can't do it.

And sometimes, it's easier to say "I can't" than "I won't." Why? Because "I can't" is the perfect escape hatch from accountability. It implies the problem is outside their control—and you can't be held responsible for something you're literally unable to do.

SARAH'S REALITY CHECK

Back to Sarah and her anxiety. She believes she is completely incapable of handling normal teenage life: going to school, hanging out with friends, becoming independent, discovering her interests, understanding herself and the world around her. When pushed to engage in these basic life tasks, her only response is "I can't."

She genuinely feels unable to do what her parents and teachers ask of her. But from the outside, it looks like she's capable of so much more than she gives herself credit for—she just "won't" push herself enough to make a difference. She "won't" acknowledge daily progress, "won't" commit to a path forward, "won't" challenge herself.

For her, she truly "can't" do any of those things. So what do you do? This is the paradox every parent of a struggling teen faces.

THE BREAKTHROUGH STRATEGY

Step 1: Validate the reality. To Sarah, the "can't" is absolutely real. It defines her experience. If you first try to convince her she actually *can* do everything expected of her, you'll start a power struggle that only ends with her feeling misunderstood and even more resistant.

Step 2: Meet them where they are. When you acknowledge this is how she experiences her life—that she really can't navigate everything expected of her—you create an opportunity for connection. You might temporarily buy into her perspective that she's not capable and the problem is "out there," but you do this only to build rapport and foster empathy. To have influence, you first need this connection.

Step 3: Set attuned and thoughtful boundaries. After you understand her perspective, you can share a boundary from that softer, clearer, more attuned place. You can even ask for her input:

"Sweetie, I'm getting how overwhelming and impossible school feels for you right now. And I'm asking you to go. You can take breaks when teachers allow it and use your coping skills—and you need to go. How can I help you with this?"

"You don't understand at all! Why would you make me do something you know I can't do? You just said it! You said I can't do it. Now you're making me do it? Why would you do that?"

"I get that you feel like you can't go. I also know you can work toward better attendance, and maybe even enjoy it. Now, how can I support you in getting there tomorrow?"

"You clearly must hate me if you're making me do something that makes me miserable. Ugh, I hate you." *Door slam.*

THE REAL CONVERSATION

Two hours later, Mom knocks on Sarah's door.

"What do you want?"

Mom enters and sits on her daughter's bed. "What's so hard about school for you? I really want to know."

And then it all comes out: the complexity of friend group drama where she never knows where she stands with anyone; the constant distraction that makes focusing in class impossible even though she desperately wants good grades; the reality that, while some friends genuinely care about her, other kids think she's weird and openly mock her panic attacks.

Sarah's mother, now understanding the daily minefield her daughter navigates, can create more informed expectations and offer more effective support moving forward. The conversation isn't a magic cure, but it's a crucial step. Her mother thanks Sarah for sharing and doesn't rush to fix everything or remind her she still needs to go to school tomorrow. She patiently listens to the depth of her daughter's pain, becoming someone who truly understands—and can therefore be trusted.

In this case, Sarah might actually be open to believing her mother's "yes you can," because her mother finally gets the gravity of what she faces. The "can't" has real potential to shift into "maybe I can."

Once you have a clear distinction between can't and won't, and understand what's actually within your child's capability and what isn't, you can create an approach that actually works.

THE SHIFT IN PERSPECTIVE

You're beginning to see your teen differently now. That angry, defiant kid who seemed determined to make their life harder is actually just someone who is scared and overwhelmed, doing their best to survive emotional quicksand.

This shift in perspective—from seeing willful defiance to recognizing genuine struggle—is the first milestone of your journey. Seeing clearly also requires something a lot of parents resist: stepping back from the desperate need to fix, solve, and rescue.

You're about to discover that one of the very things you may think is helping your kid might be what's stopping them.

CHAPTER 3

How to Help Without Helping

"Forget it. I'm not telling you anything anymore."

Your son walks away from the kitchen table where you've just spent twenty minutes explaining why his approach to the conflict with his teacher won't work. You laid out a clear plan for your son: apologize, show more respect, and maybe ask for extra credit to bring up his grade.

Solid advice. Logical steps. Total disaster. He's now convinced you don't get it, you don't get *him*, and you definitely don't think he can handle his own life.

What went wrong? And more importantly, how do you actually help without making things worse?

THE ART OF ATTUNING

To understand the inner workings of your kid, you need to tune in to their perspective. This means listening to and understanding their life experience without thinking about what you want them to do or how you want them to feel, or making them listen to you. Then, just maybe, they'll let you see—and start to let you understand—their world.

Here's another scene: You're cleaning up after dinner, and your daughter shares that her teacher has favorites in class, is hypocritical, and targets her. It's obvious she's relating to this situation in a disempowered way, which will likely just create the same dynamic with other teachers and people now and in the future.

So, what do you do? *Let her.* Let young people find their own way navigating frustrating relationships and situations. This may sound counterintuitive, like I'm asking you to abandon your parental responsibility. But getting involved at this juncture can backfire. Here's why.

WHY SOLUTIONS CAN BE SABOTAGE

Problem-solving can add to the problem. Young people rarely want their parents to come up with solutions to their problems. And parents rarely comprehend the diverse nuances of their kid's generation. These kids know far more than they are given credit for, and when their parents propose solutions they've already thought of, they see their parents as irritating, irrelevant, and emotionally tone-deaf.

When parents jump in with unwanted advice, one of three things happens:

1. They disempower their kids by wanting to be their fixer. This unintentionally sends the message that their kids are incapable of handling it themselves.
2. Parents teach their kids how not to listen and how to give advice based on one's own self-centered perspective. Kids then run the risk of doing the same thing their parents are doing except with their friends. These kids will give empty advice based on their own perspective of life instead of getting curious about their friends' experiences and perspectives.
3. Parents cause their teens to stop sharing because the teens realize the parents aren't actually curious about their experience. The parents are more interested in having their kids feel better—which will in turn make the parents feel better.

The parents' desperate attempts to regain influence backfire—because now, instead of reflecting on their life or considering new perspectives, their teens dig in their heels just to prove their parents wrong. The parents have unintentionally started a power struggle, and now the kids are more focused on winning than growing.

When parents remove the fog of their own agenda, they can actually start to see their kids.

So how do you remove the fog? How do you show up differently when everything in you wants to jump in and fix things?

THE POWER OF COMPASSIONATE CURIOSITY

Always start a conversation with curiosity—it's the doorway through which understanding passes. When you consciously don't offer solutions and instead focus on compassion-based curiosity, magic happens. You create a safe place for trust. You don't judge how your kid feels, how they see the world, or who they are.

You send a powerful message: "You've got this. I'm looking forward to watching you come up with a brilliant solution to this situation." You show you care without taking responsibility for your child's problems. Remember, these already overwhelmed young people may happily let you take over their life if you seem more invested than they are.

CURIOSITY IN ACTION

Get clear about the intention of any conversation. Most of the time, people just want to be heard. After your kid shares, ask questions fueled by genuine curiosity with the intent of understanding. If anxiety, frustration, or worry are driving your questions, don't ask them. Wait until you can get to a place where your curiosity can be genuine.

Another example:

"So Mr. Elba gave you a detention instead of giving it to your friend—who was the one actually talking, not you?"

"Yeah, isn't that bullshit? I mean, I wasn't going to rat on my friend, but it's still ridiculous that he gave me a detention! I wasn't doing anything wrong. Teachers at this school are such dicks. I hate all of them."

"All of them? That's intense. How are you going to get through this semester with an entire course load of teachers you hate?"

"I don't know. I'll probably just zone out in every class, text my friends, and watch videos on my phone."

"Well, that's honest. Really? Okay. I'll bet you'll find another way. You're too bright, authentic, and creative to just let injustices like this pass without finding a way to successfully navigate them."

"Whatever, you always say stupid stuff like that."

"Stupid stuff that might be right... Right?"

"Ugh, you're so annoying."

THE ALTERNATIVE UNIVERSE

Without that genuine curiosity, this conversation could have gone sideways fast:

"I can't believe he gave me another detention! I mean, his class is sooo boring—what am I supposed to do?!"

"Do you really think it's a good idea to goof off in class?" the parent inquires.

Tense silence.

"Are you just going to give me another lecture on personal responsibility or whatever? I mean, you always side with the teacher anyway."

Ouch.

This is exactly what happens in countless homes every day. But the beautiful thing about conversations is they don't have to stay derailed. Here's how you bring it back.

THE THREE-MOVE COMEBACK

As an insightful parent, you can do three things that most parents won't think to do:

1. **Own your part** in creating the dynamic.
2. **Ask permission** before offering your perspective.
3. **Respect the answer** you get.

Watch the same conversation take a completely different turn:

"Do you really think it's a good idea to goof off in class?" the parent asks.

Tense silence.

"Are you just going to give me another lecture on personal responsibility or whatever? I mean, you always side with the teacher anyway."

"You know what? You're absolutely right. I do automatically side with the teachers sometimes because I relate to them as adults. That's not fair to you. I think I jump in with solutions because it makes *me* feel better—like I'm fixing something—but you're not something to be 'fixed.' You're someone I care immensely about. I think I'm just trying to control a situation that isn't mine to control. That's my mistake, and I'm sorry."

"Um…okay. Yeah, that's exactly why I don't tell you stuff anymore. The more I share, the more you freak out and try to manage everything. It's annoying…and honestly exhausting."

Deep breath. "That must be so frustrating. Thank you for being so honest with me—even though it stings to hear. You're right, and I've been making things harder when I thought I was helping. I'm going to back off. But if you ever want a different perspective that might be useful, just let me know. No pressure either way."

"Yeah…maybe."

THE INVITATION

What this parent just created is something exceedingly rare in the world of the stressed parent-child relationship: an open door with no pressure to walk through it.

The parent just essentially said: *I see you, I trust you, and if you ever want my input, I'll be here.*

This isn't manipulation. It's respect wrapped in humility. And it's exactly what opens hearts that have been slammed shut.

Your job isn't to control behavior—it's to become someone worth listening to. When you give up trying to force influence, you create space for real influence to grow. *This is how you become the parent they turn to instead of the one they turn away from.*

THE UNCOMFORTABLE TRUTH

If you're feeling a bit uncomfortable right now, that's exactly right. Recognizing that your "help" might be sabotage isn't easy to face. Most parents read this chapter and think, "But if I don't solve their problems, who will? If I don't guide them in the right direction, who will?"

The answer is this: They will. But only when you stop taking responsibility for their choices and start taking responsibility for your own emotional responses to their choices.

This insight leads to a compelling question that every parent of a struggling kid must eventually face: *What if their destructive behavior isn't random chaos, but actually serves a purpose that I can't see yet?*

CHAPTER 4

Everything Serves

Naomi is intrigued by the conversation she's having with her therapist, and she begins to reflect. "I don't like so many parts of myself," she shares as she looks vacantly out the window.

"Remember what we've talked about. Every part of you is an aspect you've created, usually in response to your environment," the therapist explains. "I know so many of them are hard to look at, but it's only because they're not actually you. They're different versions of your protection—aspects you created so you wouldn't have to hurt as much. Each one has served you, and continues to serve you, by keeping you safe."

"Okay, let's run with this. How do you think the angry aspect of myself keeps me safe?"

"Alright, I'll play along. By pushing others away, you won't be hurt first."

"The ashamed one?"

"Okay, I know you know this, so I'll just remind you. Shame is distorted protection—it convinces you that you don't deserve love, so you won't have to be hurt. And it's a disguised version of arrogance. It says, 'I'm right; I'm not worthy of care. All those good things people say about me? Not true. I'm not a good person. I suck.'"

"Huh, I don't think we've talked about that. How would shame help?"

"So you won't get crushed pursuing something you think you'll never get anyway."

"Ouch. True, though. What about the overly confident part of myself?"

"Well, false pride makes you feel worthy when deep down you're convinced you're not."

"Damn. I'm going to have to think about this. Like, a lot."

Naomi's realization is the beginning of a profound shift in her understanding. But to really get how this applies to your kid, we need to explore how it plays out in their daily choices.

WHY DESTRUCTION MAKES PERFECT SENSE

Everything we do, including destructive behaviors, meets a need we have on some level. So then why do people make choices that clearly hurt them and others? The answer is both complex and devastatingly simple.

Through tens of thousands of hours working with thousands of young people and families in crisis, I've discovered one primary reason young people choose to self-destruct: *They fundamentally don't like who they are.*

It doesn't matter whether someone appears overly confident and high-achieving or they isolate and seem depressed or anxious. Destructive choices reflect how kids feel about themselves. Period. Their inner world gets projected outward into their life, so they create circumstances that make them feel how they feel about themselves: awful. Simply put, we create external circumstances that match our beliefs about ourselves.

For example, self-absorbed, "confident" people mask their own insecurities by shrinking their world. They make everything about them so they don't have to take risks. They can't tolerate being vulnerable; if they are truly seen in the intimacy of connection, they will be revealed as the fraud they know they are deep down. This self-absorbed isolation is comfortable because it's safe. People like this are some of the most lonely I've ever met. But whether people are isolating through this false confidence or more obvious withdrawal, the same deeper force is at work.

THE WOUND THAT DRIVES EVERYTHING

Every choice comes with consequences. If your kid is unaware of the negative impact their choices have on them or others, they're likely to repeat those choices. But if your kid becomes fully aware of a choice's destructive impact and continues making that same choice anyway, something crucial gets revealed about what's really going on inside them. They likely see no hope, no promise, and no ability for themselves or their world to improve.

The desire to continuously make destructive choices,

despite knowing the damage they cause, points to only one thing: a wound.

Emotional wounds left unattended fester and spread through the entire psyche. Why would someone keep choosing pain even when they know it will bring suffering to themselves and others? *Because it's familiar.* Familiarity is safe. For this person, pain equals safety.

Over time, that familiar pain becomes their comfort zone. **When you're already emotionally depleted, you don't have the reserves to take on even more discomfort, even if it might eventually lead to healing.**

These young people aren't choosing misery because they're weak or broken. They're choosing it because it's the only emotional territory they know how to navigate. Change feels impossibly risky when they're convinced they're fundamentally flawed. This is where the logic of self-destruction becomes clear—and heartbreaking.

THE CRUEL TRUTH OF SELF-SABOTAGE

Young people believe they deserve all the pain they're getting—they're not lying or being dramatic. And while they actually have fantastic qualities and a beautifully unique perspective they can share with the world, all of that feels foreign at best, and fake at worst.

Why? Because believing in their own worth is a terrifying risk. If they challenge those prevailing limiting beliefs about how awful they are and then fail at convincing themselves they have innate value, they'll have to face the devastating possibility that their worst fears about themselves might be true. Growth requires stepping into the unknown and challenging the beliefs that wounds create—but that takes courage kids who struggle simply don't have.

It's far more compelling to believe the felt experience of their misery than some far-off vision of a transformed, enjoyable life. It's easier to stay stuck in the familiar struggle than waste energy working toward something they can't imagine happening.

THE STORY THAT KEEPS THEM TRAPPED

Every wound tells a story, and young people who struggle become devoted to narratives that shield them from responsibility. When your identity forms around pain and hardship, you create a story where life happens to you, not because of you. Why bother caring about consequences or failure when nothing is within your control anyway?

But it's the wound—or rather, the protective mechanism around the wound—that drives every choice. The young person doesn't talk about the painful experiences that created the wound because vulnerability, trust, and resilience are required to bring it into the light where it can heal. Instead, the unconscious protective mechanism, which is ultimately meant to keep them safe, makes decisions moment by moment.

WHEN PROTECTION LOOKS LIKE ATTACK

From the outside, this protective mechanism can look like deliberate cruelty. When your teen lashes out, lies, or makes choices that seem designed to hurt you, it's easy to believe they're intentionally trying to cause damage. The pain feels so personal, so targeted, that it's natural to conclude they're the enemy of your peace, your family, and even their own well-being.

But it is only that their protective system is so hypervigilant, so convinced that connection equals danger, that it strikes first. The very love you're offering feels threatening to a wounded psyche that has learned love comes with conditions, disappointment, or abandonment. So they push you away before you can hurt them. They reject you before you can reject them.

Understanding this dynamic will shift how you see their behavior—and how you respond to it.

YOUR CHILD IS NOT THE ENEMY

Your kid is a good person who is hurting. Do your best not to question this. They're likely in such intense pain that they're willing to sacrifice precious aspects of their life to avoid feeling more pain.

Some parents think their kid—especially one who's aware of the consequences—is intentionally making poor choices just to hurt people. But knowing the negative impact isn't always enough to inspire change. Courageous action comes from hope, belief in yourself, and the possibility of a good outcome. Motivation doesn't emerge from a void, which is where most struggling kids live.

When you recognize that your teenager isn't fundamentally broken, you can tap into the kind of rock-solid compassion that changes everything about how you parent. Of course you're going to feel hurt, helpless, and frustrated watching them torch good things in their life while showing no regard for the devastation left behind.

But when they successfully convince you they don't deserve your love and compassion—when you start believing they really are just a selfish, destructive person—then the wound has achieved its goal. The protective mechanism wins, and the beautiful person hiding behind all that pain becomes invisible. Understanding this changes how we view every destructive choice they make.

DISTORTED WISDOM OF BAD CHOICES

Remember, everything serves. Everything. That includes poor choices and destructive behavior. Everything your kid does serves a purpose, even when their choices seem completely counterproductive or painful.

Bad choices serve by keeping them safe—safety in the familiar, the comfortable, the predictable. The brain loves what it knows. But to really grow means leaving behind the familiar and getting uncomfortable long enough to create something new.

This feels impossible for kids who struggle, because they're already drowning in discomfort from their current pain. Asking them to voluntarily enter *more* unfamiliar territory—even if it leads to healing—is like asking someone who's barely treading water to swim toward an uncertain shore.

So instead, they unconsciously choose the pain they know. Every destructive choice is actually a sophisticated decision made by a belief system designed to protect them. And this reveals a profound principle about human behavior:

The driver of every thought, feeling, and behavior serves a defined purpose. These drivers support the belief system we have about ourselves and the world—whether helpful or destructive. This is sometimes hard to understand because it requires taking responsibility for all of our choices and actions.

The upshot is if everything serves a purpose, then even the

most destructive patterns can be understood, addressed, and ultimately transformed. This understanding is the foundation for everything that follows.

THE REFRAME THAT CHANGES EVERYTHING

Some of you won't need this reminder—but some of you will: Your kid isn't your enemy. They're not trying to hurt you or others out of malice or spite. They're a wounded person whose protective mechanisms have convinced them that pain is safer than vulnerability, that isolation is safer than connection.

When you can see their struggles through this lens—as protective strategies instead of personal attacks—everything changes. The anger that feels so pointed and personal is just their way of pushing you away before you can hurt them. The lies that felt like betrayal are just their way of protecting a tender truth they don't trust you with yet.

This reframe is critical, and it raises two more important questions: Why don't they trust you? Why have they shut you out of the very place where healing happens?

CHAPTER 5

The Trust Tightrope

"You don't trust me. If you did, you'd let me spend the night at her house!"

Imagine you are this young woman's parent. She has had some previous incidents with drugs, alcohol, and sneaking out that give you compelling reasons not to let her spend the night somewhere. She explodes and calls you controlling. Then, instead of being annoyed and defending yourself for why you're making the choice you're making—thus giving her further evidence for how paranoid, reactive, and controlling you can be—you take a breath and calmly acknowledge the impact your decision has on her world.

"I get how awful this is for you and that it seems like I don't trust you."

"If you knew how 'awful' this was for me," your daughter says, making air quotes with her fingers around the words you just used, "you'd let me go! You definitely don't 'get' how bad this is. You have no idea."

"Okay, understood. Well, let me say it this way: I can understand, based on what you are saying now, how hard this obviously is for you, how terrible this is. And you know what? You're right in a way—I don't trust you to go over there yet. Because I don't trust you're going to make good decisions. I mean, remember what happened last time?"

Your daughter rolls her eyes.

"I *want* to trust you. I want to see if you can handle the level of independence you have before I give you more. Because I know you know what happened the last time you went over there. I need to wait another month or so and actually meet your friend before I feel good about you staying over with her."

"Got it. I have to earn back trust I never actually lost in the first place. Makes total sense, Mom."

Sigh. "Well, that's not exactly it, but sure. It's a no for tonight. I'll let you know when dinner is ready, sweetie."

This dance between trust and control plays out in countless homes every day. But what's really happening underneath these exchanges?

YOUR TWO-PART MISSION

Your primary responsibility as a parent is to keep your kid safe. Your second? Inspire them to trust you.

To really understand the power of trust, we have to explore its antithesis: *control*. With trust, you feel at ease, expanded, and connected. With control, you feel small but try to appear big, cutting yourself off from others. When you trust, your desperate need to control disappears.

Control is what happens when old wounds make you terrified of being hurt or betrayed again. This is why when you relate through trust, you create deeper connections; and when you relate through control, you create distance, cold responses, and the breeding ground for epic power struggles.

I know it's tempting to get into the world of wanting to control what your kid does, because they can make such bad choices, but let's explore a more effective way of approaching your parenting.

CONTROL BIRTHS DEFIANCE. TRUST DEEPENS CONNECTION.

This distinction is so important for kids who struggle because their experience of parental control can threaten their personal freedom, their power to influence their own life, and (at its most toxic level) their emotional rights. When parents operate from the energy of control, defiance is usually the result. And the remarkable thing about defiance is that, at its core, it's actually an expression of a need for connection. It shows up as anger, rebellion, or—ironically—their own need for control in the face of feeling oppressed.

TRUST, VERIFY, AND BRACE FOR IMPACT

Let's revisit the previous vignette. Your daughter wants to spend the night at a friend's house where she was caught smoking and drinking six months ago. It would be easy to just say *no* given what happened last time.

But since then, your daughter has shown better decision-making and genuine regret about the incident. You've also spent more time with her friend, and they seem like a health-oriented kid on a path of growth. There is enough evidence to support giving your daughter a shot at some independence. So you trust her to make good decisions that night. When you see her in the morning, you verify that all went well with a drug test, breathalyzer, or checking her clothes for alcohol.

Here's the key: Be transparent about your "verification" process upfront. If you choose to do that, be direct—not sneaky—about it. That's part of the agreement you'll both make going in:

I'm trusting your word, and I get to verify you're telling the truth.

Think of it as building a bridge of trust—you're both working from opposite sides toward the middle. Each successful experience adds another plank to that bridge, making it stronger and more reliable.

You have to build that bridge from your side too. That means following through on your word, your promises, and acknowledging when your kid makes good choices. You should gradually dissolve boundaries as they prove themselves mature enough to handle the independence you're giving them. If they come home on time and have not drunk alcohol or smoked, you can appreciate that they kept their word and maybe extend their curfew next time. If they're honest about a mistake they made, you can respond with appreciation for their honesty rather than just punishment for the mistake.

Your side of the bridge also means owning your mistakes. When you overreact, misread a situation, or make a parenting choice that backfires, you acknowledge it. You're modeling the vulnerability and accountability you're asking of them. Over time, as you each prove yourself trustworthy to the other, the verification can gradually fade away because the bridge is strong enough to support real trust.

By the way, saying no to a request your kid brings you may have nothing to do with being controlling. We just call that a boundary. It may *feel* like you're being controlling to them, because they may *feel* controlled when you limit what they can and can't do—but that's just called good, solid parenting.

The way to have this moment inspire trust is this: **Be transparent about why you're saying no, and don't get bothered by the fact that they are bothered.** Being reliably caring and open inspires them to trust you. Why? Because people who are emotionally reliable are emotionally trustworthy. This is how you can keep building trust in nearly every interaction you have.

This bridge-building approach transforms every interaction into a chance to strengthen trust rather than tighten control. Even when you're not ready to completely step back, you can shift from rigid control to collaborative verification. Trust deepens through this process of mutual accountability.

However, as you establish caring and thoughtful boundaries, prepare to be met with some resentment and resistance. Here's what it can look like:

"You can't just keep me as your little girl for the rest of your life! What's wrong with you? You need therapy!"

"Okay, I get it—you're pissed, you think I'm a power-hungry control freak, incapable of letting his little princess be free in this dirty cruel world. Well, you might actually be right to some degree. And this is the choice I'm making tonight."

"Ugh, you are so annoying!" *Door slam.*

You know you made the right choice. I mean, it just makes

sense not to let her go tonight...right? But then the guilt sets in, the tightening of your chest, the doubt, the wanting things to just be easier. This is what caring for someone feels like in the trenches of parenting. Your pain isn't evidence of your failure; it's proof of your love.

The fact that you sometimes question yourself reveals how invested you are in their well-being, how desperately you want to get this right. Every parent who has ever loved a child through their hardest season has stood exactly where you're standing now, feeling exactly what you're feeling. You're not failing—you're fighting for them, even when they can't see it. And sometimes, especially in those door-slamming moments, the stand you make is the most loving thing you can do.

And there's something else happening in these moments. The boundaries that make your kids furious today will become the foundation of their confidence tomorrow. The verification they resent now will teach them accountability they'll value later. And the parent they're rejecting in this moment will be the one they turn to when life gets really hard. Your willingness to endure their anger while maintaining your love is not just good parenting—it's also the kind of strength that shapes a human being. This is the truth that emerges when you understand trust as the foundation of transformation.

THE BRIDGE OF LOVE

Standing for your kid's health in moments when they don't appreciate it nurtures a subconscious form of trust in you. Their current and temporary frustration is inspired by superficial and impulsive desires whose potential consequences they can't see. Becoming someone they trust means you value who they can be more than something they want to do right now.

This is you building your side of the bridge of trust. This is how your love can reach them in both a profound and uncomfortable way. In fact, without your saying no at times like this, your love can't get to them.

You're like a gardener who has to prune branches that are still alive in order to help the tree produce the most fruit. If we asked the (teenage) tree, it certainly wouldn't understand why you're cutting away its freedom. But you know without the pruning shears of your "no," the life force scatters into weak, directionless growth that can't bear the fruit you know is possible. Your love gets expressed powerfully in the clean cuts you make. Every boundary is a deliberate choice (or best guess) that channels their life force toward something stronger, deeper, and more beautiful than they can see now.

So, building trust requires your patience, consistency, and courage to face your kid's resentment without becoming defensive. Because if you hold a boundary and then get mad about their response, you diminish the deeper meaning of why you held the boundary. You also unintentionally blame them for something you did. Being a parent means you're mature enough to deal with the consequences of the boundary you're holding. Let them be angry, frustrated, sad, dramatic, whatever—it's fine. They are responsible for dealing with how they feel about the whole situation. This is how you become someone worth trusting.

But many parents get stuck wondering: "If they won't talk to me, if they've shut me out completely, how do I begin to build or rebuild that trust?" The answer lies in understanding why they've chosen silence in the first place.

CHAPTER 6

The Sound of Silence

"How was school, Anya?"

"It sucked. The worst teacher in the school gave me an F in participation because I was, like, two minutes late to class. Mr. Harrison just hates me because of the way I dress."

She was twenty minutes late, and it's happened about ten times this month. She sometimes dresses provocatively or with so much flair it's distracting. But you don't say any of this out loud.

"Oh, that sucks. What do you plan to do about it?"

"Probably nothing, since he's such an NPC." (You don't know what "NPC" means.) "Plus, he already has his way of thinking about me that I could never change."

With everything it takes, you resist saying, *Are you kidding me?! If you just went to freaking class on time, or studied and tried your hardest, he might think differently about you! For that matter, the whole world might think differently about you, including me.*

Yeah, you're not going to say that now or probably ever. But man, it's tough to hold it in. A part of you would love to tell her how you really feel, but it's just not a good idea—at least not yet, and definitely not that way.

Why does it feel so impossible to have an honest conversation with your kids? Why do your words just bounce off of them like you're talking to an easily offended wall?

WHY YOUR VOICE GETS LOST IN THE STATIC

Young people who struggle don't listen because they aren't incentivized to. They don't experience the relief that comes with opening up to someone who really gets them. They like sharing with their friends more than you because their friends understand their world, their friends don't judge them, and their friends don't "control" them—with their friends, they are free. That experience they have with them is one you've got to find a way to honor and appreciate. Even if it seems like those relationships are toxic, your kid gets something out of them. Maybe they feel understood, safe, accepted, or things you may not even currently understand. The point is, they *want* to be connected with their friends. They may not want to be connected to you—yet.

So, don't expect your kids to listen to you. Become someone they want to listen to.

Practice speaking in a way that is compelling—a way that is direct, light, humorous, authentic, and clear. It's important we take responsibility for how we speak so they feel compelled to actually listen.

I'm sure you know people who drone on and lecture about what kids should and shouldn't do, especially when those people don't follow their own advice. The old *Take my advice, I'm not using it* tactic. Yeah, it doesn't work. Maybe you're even guilty of this yourself; most of us are. For example, you might tell them to put their phone away at dinner and then answer important work texts at the table, or you might tell them how important it is to see the best in everyone but then share how awful people are at work. These inconsistencies don't just make them tune you out—they also feed the voice that's already telling them adults can't be trusted.

Given the myriad stressors and extreme pressure kids are under to achieve and fit in, young people who struggle have far more important reasons to not listen to you than to listen. So you've got to make yourself compelling. Remember, when kids struggle, they fundamentally don't like who they are, regardless of what they tell you. They don't trust the world or themselves, and they certainly aren't internally motivated to listen to your perspective if it doesn't bring *you* joy, fulfillment, and passion.

What hope are you giving them if you aren't living your most passion-infused, fulfilling life? This brings us to an important dilemma: If you're not someone they want to listen to, why should they risk the vulnerability of sharing their private, delicate life with you?

A TIGHTROPE WITHOUT A NET

Young people don't share because they don't experience value in it. Remember, everything serves a purpose. In this case, not sharing keeps them safe, comfortable, and in a familiar world—even when that familiarity is more painful than a potentially relieving future.

If your kid doesn't share with you, it always has something to do with you. You may not be the main reason they don't share, but you at least play a role. The good news is you can do something about that. Completely unintentionally, you have likely been ineffective at creating an environment for them to be open with you.

Sometimes it isn't so much about you—sometimes something so painful has happened to them that they refuse to share because they can't bear to touch that suffering. When meaningful connection feels impossible to them, it's because some circumstance or relationship has created such overwhelming stress that they've lost hope in anyone's ability to help. Sharing requires vulnerability, and their vulnerability is like a heart chipped away by a thousand small disappointments, making even kindness from the outside feel dangerous.

HOW TO BECOME A SANCTUARY

Think of creating yourself like establishing a sanctuary. You can't force people to come in, but you can create an emotional environment so safe and welcoming that they eventually choose to trust you with their vulnerability. Here's how:

First, get rid of the pressure. Make it genuinely okay if your kid chooses not to share in every situation you wish they would. When someone knows they can come and go freely—without guilt trips or hurt feelings—they start to trust that it's actually safe. True sanctuaries never turn anyone away, and they don't make people feel guilty for leaving.

Second, lead by example. When someone in your family

shares vulnerably and you respond with appreciation rather than judgment, it creates a *magnetic pull*. On some level, they want some of that experience, but you can't expect kids to bring their wounded hearts to a place that doesn't know how to tend to them. Don't expect your kids to share meaningfully when no one has modeled what it looks like. That means you.

You can't ask your kid to seek refuge in a place you haven't been. If you want them to trust you with their real struggles, you have to show them what it looks like to share authentically without making them responsible for your emotional well-being.

If they bring something to you, and you've been doing your own emotional work to prepare for that moment, you open the potential for them to feel a relief that brings healing. And they may want to come back because that connection feels good. They'll do that when they know they'll be accepted as they are—with a gentle and light welcome, not harsh examination, interrogation, or solutions. Here's what it can look like after you've been practicing some of that inner work.

WHEN THE CONVERSATION FINALLY HAPPENS

Let's revisit our story of Anya. She is at risk of being suspended from school because of her tardiness and overall attitude.

"Anya, hey, I need to speak with you."

"Now? I'm leaving to hang with my friends right now!"

"I told you this weekend we'd be talking tonight, and I reminded you yesterday and this morning. You're not going out until we've had this talk."

"What?! You always do this! You just spring things on me last-minute and keep me from doing the only things that make me happy. I hate my life."

"All right, let me know when you're ready to start."

"I'm never going to be ready because I'm just going to be thinking about how much fun everyone is having without me. Ugh..."

"Well, I'm going to start, then. Here's the deal. The way you're living your life isn't working. It just isn't. I do my best to give you independence, to let you have your life, to let you make the choices you want to make, but you're making terrible choices that have serious effects on you, your life, and the family."

"What, so everything is my fault? Seriously? You're going to pin all of this on me? That's such bullshit."

"Whoa, that's not what I'm saying. Do you want to understand what I'm saying, or do you want to hear what you think I'm saying?"

"Fine, whatever."

"Okay, thank you. What I'm saying is that some things have to change. I'm open to your perspective on what and how, but one thing is for sure—this won't continue the way it has."

"So what? Am I grounded forever? You're going to take away my phone—again? Take away the car—again? Nothing you can do will make me change. I'm happy the way I am."

"Well, that's the first untrue thing you've said in this whole conversation."

"Are you calling me a liar?"

"Nope. I'm saying you think you're happy. I and everyone else in the family can tell you're miserable. But it's fine—you get to live however you want within reason. I can't control whether you're miserable or not, but I do have some say in how you show up in this family, in this home, and in your life, even though that last part is pretty limited."

"So what do I have to do...?"

"It's not about having to do something different. You just seem so sad, so angry, so anxious—honestly, you seem like you're drowning, and I'm not sure what I can do to help you. Because I want to, but I'm terrified to try things because I don't want to make it worse or drive you away from us. You and your brother and sister are some of the most important things in the world to me, and I know I need to do something, but I'm not even sure what."

Tears start flowing down your face, but you stay focused on Anya.

"So, what are you going to do...?" She's uneasy but starting to open up.

"I'm not sure. I'm hoping you can help me with that part."

Silence. You can tell she's starting to feel a little emotional, but then she bristles, rejecting the vulnerability that was just starting to rise inside her.

"You want me to ground myself? Forget it. You can't stop me from going to see my friends."

You pause, sigh, and wipe away your tears. "I don't want to ground you, either. I know how important it is for you to see your friends. You just seem to feel awful all the time. I never see you happy anymore."

"Well, I'm happy with my friends."

You take another deep breath. "Got it. I just don't see that, which is fine. Here's my thought: Something has to change with school. You're at risk of getting suspended for being so late and having so many problems with staff and teachers. That's one thing that has to start changing, and I want your input on what you think can happen. What do you think we should do?"

"I don't know. I guess I just need to be on time more."

Oh my gosh. Hallelujah.

THE DANCE OF CONNECTION AND STRUCTURE

Even though this conversation isn't complete and there is loads more to address and figure out, it's a good model for masterfully balancing the two most crucial aspects of parenting: **relationship and structure**. Anya's parent (you) created explicit expectations about things needing to change but kept fighting to empower Anya to have a voice in how. They were emotional and transparent about their desperation and difficulties, but they didn't dump the responsibility for those feelings on their daughter's shoulders.

Being clear, strong, and open while communicating expectations focused on collaboration and fostering independence is what drives conversations that actually change things. It's not about choosing between being supportive or firm. The magic happens when you're both at the same time. You're beginning to see your teen differently now, but the deeper transformation requires turning that same lens of understanding toward yourself.

THE MIRROR TURNS INWARD

You've learned to see your teenager differently—not as a problem to fix, but as a person to understand. You're discovering that their "won't" often means "can't," that their silence serves a purpose, and that even their most destructive choices are attempts to stay safe in a world that feels dangerous.

Understanding them is a great first step, and it's half the journey. The sometimes more difficult half—and the one that actually makes more of a difference—is understanding yourself. Because everything you've just learned about your teen applies to you, too.

Every time you felt triggered reading about James's car

meltdown, Sarah's school refusal, or Jake's explosive anger—or even if you were triggered about a certain perspective—that wasn't just about them or the idea. It was about you.

Your kid's struggles that frustrate you the most, the behaviors that make you want to shake them and yell, "Just make better choices!"—those reactions are pointing toward something unhealed in your own story.

Let's think about this: Why does their defiance feel so threatening? Why does their withdrawal make you panic? Why does their pain activate such desperate urgency in you to fix everything?

The answers aren't in their psychology. They're in yours.

Your kid's struggles aren't happening in isolation. **They're happening in relationship with you.** And until you understand your role in that dynamic, until you see how your own wounds and triggers contribute to their pain, you'll keep trying to fix them instead of healing the relationship.

You can't guide someone to a place you haven't been. You can only take someone on a journey as far as you yourself have gone. Your own depths determine how deep you can take them. You can't teach them how to be calm, regulated, or not dramatic while you're freaking out or hiding your anxiety. You can't be vulnerable if you're hiding behind your own walls. And you can't create the kind of trust that transforms relationships until you understand what's blocking your ability to trust.

Your kid's struggles aren't separate from your own. They're intimately connected with yours, woven together by invisible threads of family patterns, generational wounds, and the beautiful, messy process of two imperfect people trying to love each other well.

Let's turn the mirror inward.

PART 2

Understanding Us

Until you sit with the mirror of inner work and honestly look at your weaknesses, your insecurities, and your blind spots, you'll see others through the fog of your own unexamined experiences. What you think is *them* is just *you*, projected outward. Understand yourself first. Then you won't just see the other person—you'll *meet* them.

TIME FOR A CONFESSION

Here's something I haven't told you yet, and it might surprise you: I'm not a parent. Never have been. And I know what you might be thinking.

But before you throw this book across the room while asking *What the hell does this guy know about raising kids?* let me tell you about the moment that taught me so much of what I needed to know about mirrors, trust, and why some of my most guarded clients once felt impossible to reach.

About twenty years ago, I was in my final year of a three-year, post-graduate clinical therapy training. I loved it. I grew immensely both personally and professionally, and I was one of the senior participants in the group who occasionally took on leadership roles. During one training intensive, I was asked to take a lead on a couple of activities. I thought I was being helpful—sharing my "wisdom" and "guiding" others so they could learn what I had learned. And at the end of the weekend, I was quite satisfied and proud of how I had shown up with the new trainees and facilitators I had known for a number of years.

However, the following week, the lead trainer and founder of the program called me into his office. I thought maybe he wanted to discuss an elevated role in the program for me. But instead (and unfortunately for me), he told me about how rude I had been, how hurtful, how cruel, how insensitive, and how arrogant I had acted—especially with the newer participants. He said I essentially strutted around the room flexing about how I knew everything the trainers were teaching and how all the fellow trainees were there to learn from me. Two of the new trainees had already quit, and three others were considering leaving.

I was gutted. I was heartbroken that I had hurt people I cared about. I was mortified that I had thought he might have called me there to promote me. I couldn't believe I had actually thought I had done such a good job. And there it was—the unconscious belief I'd been trying to outrun my entire life: *I really was a failure.* I sat on his couch, completely shell-shocked with tears running down my cheeks. I shared my profound remorse while nervously wiping away my tears.

The bitter irony cut deep. In my desperate attempt to avoid being seen as inadequate, I'd overcompensated so dramatically that I'd become insufferably arrogant, blind to the very thing so many others could clearly see: *My arrogance covered my deep insecurity.* It was another lesson on how sometimes our greatest failures can become our most profound teachers.

THE MIRROR CRACKS OPEN

At the next training, I started the first session with a heartfelt apology and a tearful commitment to be better. I took ownership of how I had impacted everyone, and I explained how my deep insecurity had manifested as arrogance, thinking I knew everything, and treating people so condescendingly. All this had blinded me to how my actions actually impacted people. The group of fifty-plus participants received it well, and I went on to humbly reengage in the training and mend the relationships that were strained.

That experience began something profound in me. I started to become more authentic, more genuine, and more vulnerable. I looked more deeply at how insecure I actually was, and at how all that arrogance and confidence was just armor—thick, heavy protective shield held by a scared kid who didn't actually want to open up to anyone.

That humility—that crash into my own wounded reality—completely transformed how I connected with kids who struggled.

The next time I sat across from those guarded kids who didn't trust anyone, especially their parents or adults, I had a new insight that changed everything: **I didn't trust people, either.** I was wounded just like them. I had covered my difficult history with my parents, adults, and my own low self-esteem with arrogance and fake confidence.

Those "difficult" clients weren't difficult at all. They were mirrors. They showed me exactly what I looked like when I was protecting myself. This realization completely changed how I understood not just those kids, but also the entire therapeutic process. I dove into another layer of personal work and my own therapy to accept and acknowledge the mistrust and hurt I felt from when I was young. The humility and openness I gained during that period of transformation has stayed with me to this moment. It paved my way to more deeply understanding the kids I work with who struggle, but it also helped me understand parents who have a hard time connecting with their kids or themselves.

WHY THIS MATTERS FOR YOU

This is why I can give you parenting guidance without being a parent myself: **I've been invited into the deepest, most vul-**

nerable spaces you can imagine within families. I've sat with parents in their deepest despair and kids in their most brutal pain. I've seen patterns that parents are too close to notice, and wounds that mirror each other across generations.

My role as a "professional outsider" has given me something unique—I get to see what you can't see when you're in the thick of it. When your teenager is pushing every button you have, when you're triggered and reactive, when you're caught in the same argument for the hundredth time—I can see the dance you're both doing because I'm not dancing it with you.

But more importantly, working with these kids has forced me to examine every corner of my own psyche. Every time I got frustrated with a kid for just being a kid who struggles, every time I wanted to shake them and say "Stop doing that!"—that was my cue to look in the mirror. To turn inward.

Here's what I discovered: What we see in them is always, always about us.

That angry, defiant kid who just won't listen? They're showing us our own relationship with authority. That anxious kid who won't take risks? They're reflecting our own lack of courage. That kid who seems to lie about everything? They're mirroring our own struggles with trust and authenticity. *Here's a tenet of transformation: If you didn't get so deeply triggered by the issues your kid is grappling with, you wouldn't have work to do in that area.*

This is the Mirror Principle that can transform everything for you: **Until you can see your own wounds clearly, you'll keep trying to fix theirs.** And it never works. Ever.

Your kid isn't your problem to solve. They're your guide, showing you exactly what needs healing in yourself.

THE GAZE TURNS

This is the first stage of your own transformation. You're starting to see your kid not as a problem to be solved, but as a person to be understood. You're recognizing that what looks like defiance is actually pain, and what feels like rejection is actually protection.

And this shift in perspective can change everything. When you see your kid's behavior as communication rather than manipulation, when you understand their silence as safety-seeking instead of punishment, you stop taking their struggles personally and start responding from love instead of fear. You're doing the hardest work many parents never even attempt. Well done.

The question that guides the next stage of your journey is this: How might your own unhealed wounds, unconscious patterns, and emotional triggers be contributing to the very struggles you're trying to help your kid overcome?

CHAPTER 7

Is It Me, or Is It Them?

Brad refuses to do chores, ditches school, and won't touch homework—all just to punish his parents. And he readily admits it.

His mother sits across from me, exhausted. Dark circles under her eyes tell the story of sleepless nights spent wondering where she and Brad's father went wrong. His father stares at the floor, jaw clenched, trying to hold back years of frustration.

"We've tried everything," Brad's mother whispers. "Consequences, rewards, therapy, taking everything away. Nothing works. It's like he wants to destroy his life just to hurt us."

She's not wrong. That's exactly what Brad wants.

WHEN SPITE BECOMES A LIFESTYLE

For Brad, what started as a power struggle over the tiny details of teenage life has snowballed into a spiteful way of living. His parents overcorrected with an elaborate system of punitive chores and restrictions built on the idea that he had to "learn how to take responsibility."

Brad was living a shell of an existence—stripped of phone privileges, video games, and friends. He occasionally snuck out and got high, but then he would get caught, get punished, and the brutal cycle would repeat.

The maddening part is that Brad could have stopped this cycle quite easily. But due to the complex web of his troubled psychology, he wasn't able to do anything different. Meanwhile, his parents were caught up in their own triggers, completely unsuccessful in getting through to him.

The war began over one specific battleground: Brad's friends. He loved them. His parents hated them. For Brad, his friends were there for him no matter what—not like his family who punished him, judged him, and caged him. "Those kids are from broken homes, are drug users, and are going nowhere in life," they'd say to Brad in hopes of convincing him to not see them.

And there it was. They hated what he loved. **Influence is created by connection. When there's no connection, influence gets weaponized by whoever has the most power.** In this case, it was Brad. Brad was willing to go farther than his parents in order to win this power struggle. He would sacrifice the most important aspects of his life (school, well-being, freedom), in order to make his point: *You can't control me.*

A month after our first session, Brad's parents called me in a panic. He'd been arrested for possession of cannabis. As they drove to the police station at 2:00 a.m., his mother finally asked the question she'd been avoiding: "What if this isn't about him? What if we're a part of the problem?"

It was the most relevant question she'd asked in years.

THE MIRROR WE DON'T WANT TO LOOK INTO

That question—"What if we're a part of the problem?"—is where lasting transformation begins. It's also the point where most parents want to run away. But if Brad's story feels familiar, if you recognize that dynamic of escalating power struggles and mutual destruction, you're not alone, and there are clear steps you can take to remedy it.

Here's what I've discovered while working with thousands of families who experienced moments like this: The patterns you see most clearly in your kid are usually the ones you're blind to in yourself. Your inner state directly impacts your teen's inner state. The most powerful and most destructive aspects of yourself are the ones you're least aware of. *And we pass on to others what we don't see in ourselves.*

Does some part of you get bothered when your kid breaks a rule, doesn't do homework, lies to you, or does the million other things most teenagers do? If so, it's okay; all of that can be objectively frustrating. When this frustration happens a lot, though, it means you're reacting from your own wounded places.

THE MIRROR TEST

Look at unhelpful patterns that exist in your kids—they can be victims to their world, they give up too easily, they don't do things that are hard but good to do, they're quick to react and judge others, they live attached to their phones, they're stubborn and self-absorbed, or they aren't willing to see how they contribute to their problems.

The hard part is now looking at how you have those same patterns inside of you. They probably don't manifest in the same way, but rest assured, they're there. Maybe instead of being attached to your phone, you distract yourself from feeling discomfort in other ways. Maybe you don't gossip like your kids, but you silently judge other people or are very hard on yourself. Or maybe you don't blame other people or circumstances so passionately and obviously as your kids, but you still find yourself stuck in the same unfulfilling relationships, dynamics, or circumstances in your life—and somewhere you might be tired of it. If part of you bristles at even considering this possibility, then it might be a confirmation those patterns exist in you.

THE UNIVERSAL FAMILY TRUTH

In every family who is stuck, **parents deny within themselves the same qualities the kid struggles with.**

Here are some examples:

The Righteous Dad: A middle-aged dad scrolls through political news and his jaw tightens. Those politicians with their arrogant, know-it-all attitudes make his blood boil. He storms into the kitchen, muttering about "idiots running the country." What can't he see? He's just as righteous and as convinced of his own moral superiority as the politicians are. He unintentionally teaches his son that being judgmental and righteous is more important than self-reflection or seeking to understand.

The Judging Mother: A mother drops her daughter off at school and notices other parents in luxury SUVs. She thinks they are judging her for having a modest sedan—but they're not. She just isn't aware of how judgmental she is toward herself, and how much she puts that out into the world around her. Her daughter absorbs this defensiveness and learns to assume others are always criticizing her—and she, too, learns to be highly critical of herself.

The Judgey Grandmother: A grandmother explains to her granddaughter how important it is to accept people as they are. "Don't judge others, honey," she says. Twenty minutes later, the granddaughter overhears her grandmother whispering on the phone about how "dramatic and immature" her granddaughter is. The granddaughter feels the sting of her judgment and learns that even people who say they love you can hurt you. She learns not to trust people's love.

We project onto the world what we refuse to see within ourselves. And as a parent, you unintentionally pass on the rejected parts of yourself to your kids.

When I shared these examples with Brad's father, his face grew pale. "The righteous father," he said quietly. "That's me. I get angry about everything—traffic, people at work, and yep, politics. And obviously I'm always pissed at Brad. And, you know, he's angry all the time, too—just like me, but in different ways."

His wife nodded slowly. "And I know my anxiety makes me harsh and hard to be around sometimes. And Brad is just like this, oh my gosh. When he used to talk to us, he would tell us how anxious he was—and now he's just become so...distant and harsh. This is tough to see."

This kind of awareness, knowing that you bear some responsibility for your kid's struggles, can be brutal. So please, practice some compassion for yourself in these and other moments. Let the fact that you're doing something about it reflect your dedication and your profound care for them. Just as your kid is navigating a challenging journey, so are you. These moments are critical opportunities that take courage. So well done, and let's keep going.

Brad's parents are turning a monumental corner—they are starting to be willing to see their own patterns mirrored in their son. It is a huge step toward healing their kid and the entire family dynamic. But for many parents, this awareness brings up an uncomfortable question: *How did I get this way when I swore I'd be different?*

THE "NEVER LIKE MY PARENTS" TRAP

This pattern becomes even more complex when parents actively try to do the opposite of what their own parents did. Many new parents swear they will never be like their parents, but they don't examine how their upbringing affected them.

One parent was raised by cold, distant, authoritarian parents. Determined to be different, they became permissive and understanding. But every time their kid misbehaves, they can't help getting angry because their kid "doesn't follow the rules." So the parent avoids their anger by not holding boundaries, thus allowing increasingly poor behavior.

Now, their kid doesn't believe in their boundaries when they do hold them because the parent lacks conviction. The parent isn't present when they hold boundaries because they are spending energy on not being angry—instead of putting focus on being emotionally present. The parent gets frustrated when gentle correction doesn't work and then gets angry (again)—just like their own father.

In this case, the child can become dysregulated because (1) the parent never taught emotional resilience through their living example, and (2) the parent doesn't give compelling reasons to follow boundaries because they're emotionally dishonest (they act calm but are actually angry).

You can't heal what you won't feel. You can't change what you won't see. And you can't give your kids what you don't have yourself.

This parent was so sincere in their attempt to be a different kind of parent than what they had. To give something different than what they received. But without looking in the mirror of self-reflection, their efforts have fallen heartbreakingly short. Given this, let's explore those blind spots—those emotional triggers—so you can actually become the parent you've always wanted to be.

YOUR TRIGGERS ARE YOUR TEACHERS

Emotional triggers can be both your worst enemy and your best friend. They're neon signs pointing to internal obstacles that block your connections with others. **The ways your kids trigger you illuminate a path toward your own evolution.**

Most parents, when they reach this recognition, do one of two things: They either shut down in shame ("We've ruined our kid.") or they deflect in anger ("This is psycho-babble nonsense—it doesn't apply to me.").

Brad's parents did neither.

"So what do we do?" his father asked. "How do we fix this?"

"I know this is going to sound cliché," I shared, "but it's true. You don't fix it; you feel it. Your triggers aren't your enemy. They are your roadmap to freedom." They both gave a little chuckle, bringing a welcome respite to the emotional intensity of the session. "Okay, that's a bit dramatic, but it's also true. The more you can first navigate the mess of uncomfortable feelings you're experiencing, the more you can actually start to parent this awesome kid the way he needs to be parented."

When parents avoid this path by making everything about their kid's issues, their kid becomes a scapegoat for the family's dysfunction and acts out even more. It's like they're screaming, "This isn't just about me!"

Most parents miss the fact that kids who struggle aren't

inspired to change. If they were, they would have already. When you become genuinely reflective about your own inner workings, you give your kid something precious—the chance to be inspired by you.

And you can't do this just for them. You have to do it for you. When you do it for you, you unlock the ability to inspire and influence your kids.

THE INSIDE JOB

So look inside. Practice being reflective. See what emotionally triggers you about what your kid does. Notice how this might relate to your own childhood, your own struggles that your child is now mirroring. Get help with this from skilled people who can see what you can't, people who can compassionately point out to you how you're unintentionally contributing to the struggle.

Remember, a child's roots can only reach as deep as the parent's soil has been tilled.

Brad's parents began the hardest work of their lives. His father started therapy to address his own anger. His mother joined a support group to address her anxiety. They stopped hyper-focusing on Brad's behavior and started focusing on their own feelings.

The change wasn't immediate. For weeks, Brad tested them harder, as if sensing their old patterns were shifting. But something was different. When he raged, his dad practiced staying calm—genuinely calm, not white-knuckling it. When Brad pushed boundaries, his mom started to respond with clarity instead of panic.

"It's like they're becoming different people," Brad told me a couple months later. "I don't know how to fight them anymore. They're not fighting back."

Your parental influence is greatest when you're aware of your own emotional state and how you're contributing to the relationship dynamic. When you take responsibility for your emotional state and its impact on others, you create the possibility for freedom not just for yourself, but also for everyone around you.

THE TRANSFORMATION

Six months after that 2:00 a.m. phone call, Brad's parents sat with me again. But this time, Brad was with them—by choice.

"I still think some of their rules are stupid," he said, grinning slightly. "But they're different now. They're not trying to control me anymore. They're just...being themselves. And I guess I like who they actually are."

This is what becomes possible when you stop trying to fix your kid and start healing yourself. **Your job isn't to eliminate their struggles—it's to become the kind of person worth struggling alongside.**

Think of it this way: You're the gardener, not the plant. You can create perfect soil, provide water and sunlight, remove weeds—but you can't force the plant to grow.

THE HEART OF IT

Brad graduated high school and went to a local university. He calls his parents every week, comes home for weekends, and is doing great overall. And this isn't all happening because he finally started to obey the rules; it's because his parents finally got themselves to start growing alongside him.

"The weird thing," his mom told me recently, "is that we were so focused on saving him, we didn't realize he was actually trying to save us. It's like his acting out was his way of saying, 'Something's wrong here, and it's not just me.'"

Your triggers aren't your enemy—they're your teachers. Every time your child pushes your buttons, they're holding up a mirror showing you exactly what needs healing in yourself. You can't control your kids. You can only inspire them.

This understanding—that influence comes from inspiration, not control—can shift everything about how you create structure in your teenager's life. Because the boundaries that really make a difference aren't the ones that control behavior; they're the ones that inspire growth.

Your kid's struggles aren't separate from your own—they're intimately connected. And **when you heal your part, you give them permission to heal theirs**.

Your kid's freedom starts with your own.

CHAPTER 8

What Drives Our Struggles

A young woman passes a guy on a busy Manhattan street and says, "Nice jacket."

What's driving the comment? Appreciation? Jealousy? Judgement?

The tone says it all—but what drives the tone? **Emotion.**

She might genuinely like the style and be giving a compliment or flirting with him. Or she might have snidely said "Nice jacket" with a smirk, just loud enough for him to hear and feel the sting of her judgement.

Why she said what she said isn't as important as what drove her to say it.

The point is: How we show up is driven by how we feel.

This simple truth has profound implications for every relationship in your life—especially the one with your kid who struggles.

THE HIDDEN DRIVERS OF EVERYTHING

This may sound basic, but most people look past this simple chain reaction: **How you act is based on how you feel. How you feel is based on how you think. How you think is based on what you believe.**

When you become aware of what drives how you think, feel, and act, you unlock something incredibly powerful—the ability to consciously create your life instead of being tossed around by your emotions like a ship in a storm.

Most people miss the fact that there's an emotional engine running beneath every thought and action. Nothing you do is emotionally neutral. The key is becoming aware of what's driving your internal experience.

When you become aware of the hidden driver, you gain the ability to create the life you actually want instead of just reacting to whatever gets thrown at you. You can navigate difficulties in ways that reduce their impact over time rather than letting them accumulate into bigger problems. This leads to a radical but liberating truth.

YOU ALWAYS HAVE A CHOICE

Remember, every struggle is an expression of an external and/or internal challenge. Understanding why you struggle unlocks a completely new way of relating to yourself, your life, and especially your kids.

It's easy to relate to suffering as if it's some mysterious force beyond our control. But here's a simple truth that might sting a little: **We choose to suffer or not.**

We don't necessarily get to choose our circumstances. We don't get to choose how people treat us or the choices other people make. But one of the great freedoms of life is that we get to choose our state—how we think, how we feel, and how we act.

Most of us don't relate to being able to think how we want, feel how we want, or act how we want. But all of these are manifestations of our mind, and **our mind is trainable**. It can be coached and molded to respond to the world around us in the ways we want it to.

How do we know this? Great thinkers and leaders have shared this approach as the key to their success, their ability to influence, and their ability to achieve their goals. There are countless examples of people who refused to tolerate the state of their life, so they dedicated themselves to improving it. And at the end of this journey to accomplish the profound tasks they set out to complete, they all found that **the state of their mind was reflected by every result they got**. Our mind creates the world around us, and the mind is created by us. So, if you don't like your life, look at the state of your mind.

THE PATH TO FREEDOM

You might be thinking, "Okay. That's nice information, J, but how does it relate to parenting my kid who is struggling?" Well, transformation in you directly translates to transformation in them, so stay with me just a little longer on this topic, and I promise it will be worth it.

How does someone actually make a shift from unconscious reaction to conscious choice? From confused suffering to practicing inspired ownership? From "things just happen to me" to "I have the potential to create my life experience"? The process follows a predictable pattern.

Here's how transformation happens.

First, a person suffers so much that they get to a breaking point. They realize only they can change who they are and how they live. They refuse to tolerate the current, limited results of their life. Then, eventually, they discover this truth: Their life only reflects how they think, feel, and act. So they pivot their gaze inward.

After examining and transforming the state of their mind, the results of their life begin to shift. And as one great teacher has shared: **"Show me your results, and I'll show you how you think."** But how do you actually develop this kind of self-mastery?

THE POWER OF AWARENESS

This transformation sounds profound, but the steps to achieve it are deceptively simple. It all comes down to one powerful practice: *awareness.*

Every moment is an opportunity to make one pivotal choice: **to become aware**. If someone cuts you off while driving and you get pissed, you can't do anything about that anger if you're unaware of it.

Most people live completely disconnected from their own emotional experience. They get angry because events happen *to* them, and without awareness, they carry that anger into the next situation. They're dragging an increasingly heavy bag of emotional burdens into every situation and relationship, ultimately passing them on to their communities, friends, partners, and kids.

But here's what makes us as humans different from every other being on the planet: We can become aware.

Let's take the same driving example. When someone does something dangerous and you get angry, you become aware of the anger. With a moment of reflection, you might realize you became angry because you felt you and your passengers were at risk.

Then you choose to do something about that emotional awareness. Because you've become aware of your current experience, you now have the power to shift it. As you practice this awareness more consistently, you'll start to notice something potentially uncomfortable or potentially liberating.

IT'S ALWAYS ABOUT US

You'll notice most of your emotional reactions aren't really about what's happening around you right now. We get angry, sad, jealous. We expect people to behave in certain ways, and we make them responsible for our emotional state. It's not that this is wrong and another way is right—it's just that **it's not effective** in supporting us in creating the life we actually want to have.

When we get upset, stressed, helpless, or depressed, we say it's because of how the world exists around us. But it isn't the world—**it's us**. Period.

Suffering exists nowhere except within our own experience.

You might still be wondering why we are talking so much about personal transformation when this is a book about how you can help your kid who is struggling. Well, here it is:

Your kid's liberation depends on your awareness. The unreflective parent is one of the greatest threats to a teenager's development.

Your self-awareness has the potential for your kid to create the life they want. Your lack of awareness creates roadblocks to their destiny and increases the likelihood of their struggle. Your lack of awareness hurts instead of helps.

The most common and destructive pattern in parents of kids who struggle is this: **They don't recognize themselves in their kids.**

The stubbornness, the lack of resilience, the closed-mindedness, the anxiety, the self-centeredness—**they all have their origin points within the parent. Always.** Like before, this realization is either devastating or liberating, depending on how you choose to use it.

THE REFLECTIVE PARENT

This shift from blaming circumstances to taking responsibility is what separates effective parents from struggling families.

The reflective parent patiently and humbly examines this truth. They're curious about how both they and their kid developed these patterns. They're receptive to feedback from therapists, counselors, mentors, and friends. They start to notice when they get annoyed, escalated, bothered, or depressed. They realize how ineffective they've become as parents and how they unintentionally reinforce the troubling patterns within their kids.

Awareness is curative and liberating—not only for you, but also for everyone you influence.

When you do your own inner work, you stop unconsciously passing on your emotional baggage to your kid. You become the kind of parent who inspires instead of triggers.

Remember, your kid's freedom starts with your own.

THE HIDDEN FORCE

You're beginning to see how your inner world shapes your outer experience—and how that directly impacts your kid. When you're triggered and reactive, your kids become defensive and distant. When you're centered and aware, space opens for real connection.

A lot of parents get stuck here. They understand it intellectually, but they keep falling into the same patterns. They know they should stay calm during conflicts, but they get pulled into power struggles. They know they should listen without judgment, but they can't help trying to fix everything.

So why does this happen? Because knowledge isn't enough. Most parents know what they should do, but unconscious patterns keep sabotaging their best intentions. And two patterns sabotage parents more than any others.

CHAPTER 9

Rescuing and Problem-Solving

A dad picks up his daughter from school and, as usual, asks about her day.

She sighs (as usual) and says, "It was fine."

"Come on..." he says. She then begrudgingly shares about friendship drama, stupid boys in her class, and how tired she is. The father pauses for a moment (without actually reflecting on how he feels, even though he's irritated because all she does is complain).

This dad then kindly offers suggestions on what she could do to make her situation better. He anxiously pats her hand and says it will be okay. His daughter withdraws her hand, rolls her eyes behind her oversized sunglasses, and, as usual, puts in her earbuds.

They ride silently home (as usual).

THE WELL-MEANING SABOTAGE

Sadly, another precious and exceedingly rare potential point of connection is lost because this dad isn't practicing becoming aware of how his subconscious patterns influence his relationship with his daughter. This well-meaning and likely kindhearted father is just trying to give some advice from what he has learned in his own life—likely from his dad. But it only pushes her away.

He relies on solving problems, offering unsanctioned advice, and subtly and unintentionally criticizing her choices as a way of connecting with her. Obviously, it's not working.

Awareness is curative, and a lack of it is toxic. When you're blind to your own patterns of thinking, feeling, and acting—and don't explore their effects on those around you—you risk creating problems or making them worse.

Unreflective people don't realize that the way they treat people is actually an extension of how they feel inside, not how people want to be treated. For example, someone might love to cheer people up or fix people's problems. On the surface, this seems genuine and caring. But dig deeper and you may find that their true motivation is to make themselves feel better by helping others feel better. If someone is anxious, then they feel anxious. If someone is angry, they get afraid.

If the other person feels fine, then they don't have to sit with their own discomfort about that person's pain. If the other person doesn't feel fine, they are confronted by their own discomfort, and their need to "fix" drives their thoughts, feelings, and actions. And unfortunately, that's manipulative—unintended, but manipulative nonetheless. This is how unconscious self-absorption works, and it can be especially destructive to the parent-child relationship.

Here's another pattern: We say things to others based on what we wish people had said to us, not what they actually want to hear. We give the comfort and advice we never received.

Without being curious about our own emotional patterns and needs, we impose them onto others without their permission. We think we're helping, but we're actually just projecting our own unfulfilled emotional desires onto them.

The result? Conflict. People can sense when you're not really seeing them—when you're seeing your own reflection instead. This dynamic plays out in countless subtle ways, but one pattern is particularly destructive for parents of kids who struggle.

THE RESCUING TRAP

The story of our dad illustrates a broader pattern that most loving parents fall into: rescuing. Understanding the difference between helping and rescuing is crucial if you want to be an effective parent.

Rescuing means you're saving your kid from experiencing some kind of emotional discomfort, and it is always well-intended but rarely necessary. If it's necessary to save a young person from a potentially dangerous situation, we call that intervening—an essential aspect of parenting.

Let me tell you a story from my own life that illustrates this well.

The year is 1986. I'm nine years old and in fourth grade. One crisp fall Sunday, I realize I've left an essential book at school that I need to complete an assignment. I start freaking out. I'm desperate to get the book so I don't get in trouble or get a zero on the assignment.

My mom tries to console me by saying it'll be okay, but I'm relentlessly frantic. We live one block from my elementary school, so I beg her to go there with me and find a way into the school to get my book. My mom is a teacher and administrator in the district—and I plead with her to find a way in so I can get the book.

She holds the line for a while but eventually gives in to my desperate tears. We go to the school at 3:00 p.m. on a Sunday and remarkably, there's a car in the parking lot. My mom and I start banging on windows and doors to get the attention of whoever's inside. After twenty minutes, a custodian comes to the door and asks what the problem is. My mom explains I've left a book in my locker and asks if I can run in and get it.

The custodian is initially hesitant but then sees me with my dried tears and desperation. He smiles and opens the door. I sprint to my locker, retrieve the book, hug his leg on my way out, and joyfully thank my mom. I return home, finish the assignment, and all is well.

Or is it?

WHAT I REALLY LEARNED

First, let's be clear: No one did anything "wrong" here—especially my beloved mom. We're not here to cast blame. This is about examining the anatomy of rescuing.

On the bright side, I learned that if I really put my mind to something, I can get it. I learned I have the ability to influence people. I learned to plan better and bring things home that I need.

On the not-so-bright side, I also learned that I could get my way even when it meant not experiencing the natural consequences of my choices. I learned that if I'm uncomfortable enough and express it compellingly, someone will get me what I want. I grew a pattern of selfishness and entitlement that bled far beyond childhood and into my twenties.

I had romantic relationships where the primary needs revolved around me. They were brief and intense, and they ultimately hinged on my own desires. They lacked meaningful depth. I was largely unreflective, so I created conflict by bringing people into my struggle. All because I wouldn't look inside. Thinking back, I can see how this single pattern shaped years of my life.

THE HIDDEN COST OF RESCUING

Now, it's not like my mom getting me a book when I was nine turned me into a complete dick. She was unwaveringly supportive for every out-of-the-box choice I made in my life (thanks, Mom).

But this vignette represents a larger pattern my parents taught me. Things that happened to me weren't my fault. I didn't have to consistently experience the uncomfortable results of my choices. So it sometimes felt like an injustice when I did. I didn't build a lot of emotional resilience from having to feel the burn of my missteps and navigate them myself.

I expected the world to give me what I wanted even if I hadn't earned it. I expected more money from jobs, more flexibility from supervisors, more understanding from romantic partners. When I didn't get what I wanted, I blamed outside circumstances and people—not myself. I was a victim of circumstance rather than a creator of my life experience.

If this pattern sounds familiar—if you recognize traces of entitlement or victimhood in your own kid—it's worth examining whether well-intentioned rescuing might be contributing to their struggles. The question isn't whether you love your kid enough to help them; it's whether you love them enough to let them experience the discomfort that builds powerful resilience.

But how do you distinguish between appropriate support and unhelpful rescuing in real time, especially when your kid is in distress?

THE REAL QUESTIONS TO ASK

It comes down to examining your motivations and asking yourself some honest questions about the situation.

Rescuing is about saving someone from their discomfort—which they can likely handle. It's fueled by your own discomfort or your perceived belief in someone's incapability. When you first address your own discomfort, navigate it, and *then* evaluate the situation, you become much more effective as a parent.

Ask yourself:

- Can my kid handle this?
- What are the short-term and long-term consequences of my lack of intervention?
- How will they learn by my lack of intervention?
- If I intervene, how will I impact their emotional resilience?

These questions will help you distinguish between rescuing and genuine support. Here's another equally unhelpful pattern many parents fall into.

THE PROBLEM WITH PROBLEM-SOLVING

Rescuing isn't the only way well-meaning parents unintentionally break connection. A close cousin of rescuing is unsolicited problem-solving.

Parents solving kids' problems is, well, a problem. Problem-solving is usually an unconscious strategy parents use to "help" their kids.

And nothing's wrong with offering advice if:

1. kids actually want to hear it,
2. the advice comes from genuinely wanting to help,
3. you're not emotionally attached to their acceptance of your advice,
4. the solutions aren't a disguised way of trying to connect, and
5. the solutions aren't a way of avoiding your own emotional discomfort.

Other than those few criteria, no big deal!

Here's the real issue, though: More often than not, parents solve problems because it's an easy, comfortable, familiar way of creating connection and influence. The intent is almost always sincere—parents want to help their kid improve their life. But the strategy is usually poorly received, the intent is often misinterpreted, and at worst, the advice is disruptive and counter to the sincere desire to connect or influence.

THE TRUST VIOLATION

When a parent gives advice without the kid's clear agreement, parents create a subtle but notable violation. Problem-solving inspires mistrust. Why? Because the parent isn't being honest.

Parents ask questions to seemingly better understand their kid and the situation, and the young person believes this—initially. But when the parent takes that information, processes it on their own, and then proposes solutions that come across as condescending and disconnected, it destroys any faith the teenager had that the parent is actually there to help.

The profoundly unaware parent can even ask questions based solely on the unconscious desire to make themselves feel better. If their kid solves their problems with the parent's "help," then the parent gets to feel good about themselves. But helping parents feel good isn't their child's responsibility—it's their own. These parents unintentionally use their kids as emotional pick-me-ups, and sometimes the kids even play along. This limits the parents' ability to become resilient and emotionally responsible. More importantly, it stops their kids from coming up with thoughtful, creative solutions to their challenges. They often grow up emotionally stunted and can lead drama-filled, unstable, and ultimately unfulfilling lives. So yeah, don't be one of those parents.

WHY WE DO THIS TO OURSELVES

So why do loving, intelligent parents keep falling into these patterns when they clearly don't work? The answer lies in understanding what's really driving their need to fix and rescue.

Usually, parents rescue and problem-solve to avoid an uncomfortable emotional experience within themselves. Though the obvious source is the child's struggle, rescuing them is actually avoiding the parents' own struggle.

Parents are anxious about what's being discussed, afraid of the outcomes, and nervous about what will happen when their kid applies the same unhelpful strategy to higher-stakes situations. *If my daughter doesn't learn to navigate these conflicts with friends and teachers now, she won't have friends and won't be successful in college. I have to help her!*

In a way, this parent is right—their daughter does need to help. But not by disguising their unintentionally righteous, condescending, desperation-fueled advice with a pleasant, calm veneer that she didn't ask for.

PUT ON YOUR OWN OXYGEN MASK FIRST

These patterns highlight the profound importance of knowing yourself. Check in with yourself before difficult conversations. When times are stressful, connect with people who can support you and tell you hard truths you need to hear.

There's a reason every airline asks parents to put on their oxygen masks before they help with their kid's. They want you to take care of yourself first so you can then take care of your kids. Do that emotionally and you'll start to see wonderful results in how your kids relate to you—they may even take your advice because you're "taking it," too.

THE FAITH FACTOR

When parents try to save kids from challenging circumstances they might be able to navigate themselves, it demonstrates a lack of faith in their kids. And on some level, they can feel it.

Young people aren't inspired to be vulnerable and share their lives with you if they sense you question their ability to be resilient. Your doubt becomes a repelling force, pushing them to seek understanding elsewhere rather than risk your disappointment. Or perhaps worse, they become the emotionally fragile person you see.

Remember: Connection breeds influence. Rescuing and problem-solving sever connection.

So, how do you break these deeply ingrained patterns?

WHAT TO DO INSTEAD

First, as always, become aware of your own emotional state. Like, right now. Yep, take a minute and just reflect on how you're feeling right now. Okay, awesome. Well done. Now do this a lot more often than you currently do—especially when things are hard. For example, are you aggravated because your kids aren't doing enough to make their life better? Are you hopeless and desperate about their future? Is the struggle they are having highlighting some other difficulty you're having in your life?

Distinguish what is about you, and what is about them. Deal with those experiences independently. Then you can be more available for meaningful conversation focused on connecting with your kid.

GETTING PERMISSION TO HELP

Remember this: The gateway to helping is getting permission. Many parents leap over the gate of their child's inner world with righteous indignation, waving the valiant sword of solutions and the impenetrable shield of protection, and then wonder why their kids are so angry and defiant.

These young people are protecting their inner world from trespassers who haven't earned or requested permission to travel in the tender workings of their psyche or their precious private lives.

The best thing you could possibly do when addressing challenges with your kid? Ask if you can help, or tell them how you'd like to help. Then do nothing. That's right. Just wait. Patiently.

Stay emotionally available for when they might actually let you into their world—even if it's just for a moment. They might kick you out before you've barely stepped inside, but remember they opened the door. Be grateful for that moment of trust, not desperate for more time inside their world.

WHEN THEY ACTUALLY ASK

If they welcome your perspective, don't think your primary goal is imparting wisdom. When they ask for guidance, your "wisdom" can be expressed in a humble sharing. "When I face circumstances like this, I practice doing my best to be curious, even though it would be easier to rush to judgement. I mean, people like that are easy to dislike and find annoying. And while I definitely get annoyed, I do find that the more I practice being patient and curious, the better the result is."

You might help your kid see the results of their choices from your perspective—which doesn't mean it's the "right" one, by the way. "It seems like whenever you get stressed, you are late to class. And you seem more stressed the more you pack everything into your free time. Don't you just want to chill sometimes? I mean, that's just how I see it. What do you think?"

Here's the paradox that trips up most parents: The more genuinely humble you are about your perspective, the more likely your kids are to actually consider it. The more pushy or proud you are, the less likely they are to hear you at all.

When you come from control, people immediately sense a power grab and fight back, because they feel like they are going to be shackled by your opinion. But when you come from humility and vulnerability, you are creating an open invitation for them to come and go, to agree or not, to do what you've done or do it their own way. And usually when parents have implemented this strategy, their kids integrate the parent's feedback and create a beautifully unique approach that could only have come from the combination of a humble parent and a courageous kid.

Think of it this way: Vulnerability is magnetic—it draws people in and repels arrogance. For a young person to take on a perspective different from their own, especially from someone with more power, they're taking a risk. And taking risks requires trust.

And you can't demand trust. You can only earn it.

THE GOLDEN OPPORTUNITY

If you get the gem of an opportunity to share your perspective with your reluctant, struggling kid, **be humble and grateful**. They have momentarily passed you the keys to their own prison cell and may even have allowed you to slide open the door.

Don't waste the opportunity with arrogant, empty advice you don't follow, based on your own poorly veiled insecurity. Share something meaningful, transparent, humble, and vulnerable, and see what happens.

If they completely disagree, good. Let them. Resist the urge to defend yourself when they say "That's not how it is at all" or "You don't know anything" or "You're so old."

Take a deep breath and remember you're secure in who you are. Just because your child disagrees with your perspective, that doesn't make you (or them) wrong. Let them know it's okay if they disagree and that you're grateful for the opportunity to share and hear their perspective.

Can you walk away from the conversation feeling good about yourself even if they rejected everything you said? Can you feel good about how you showed up authentically instead of being devastated that they didn't take your advice?

In that moment of authentic connection—even if it ended in disagreement—you showed them something powerful. You showed them what it looks like to share vulnerably without being attached to the outcome. *You demonstrated that love doesn't require agreement.*

And maybe, just maybe, the next time they're facing a difficult decision, they'll remember not what you said, but how you made them feel when you said it. *It felt...good.* Which usually means they felt connected and appreciated for who they were in that moment. They'll remember that you were secure enough to be vulnerable, and humble enough to let them disagree.

That's how real influence is built—not through perfect advice, but through imperfect connection.

This shift from fixing to connecting is profound, but it's not always easy to maintain.

WHEN GOOD INTENTIONS GO SIDEWAYS

If you're recognizing yourself in these patterns, it's okay. Every parent who loves their kid has fallen into the rescuing and problem-solving traps.

You're starting to see your own patterns clearly now—how your need to help might actually not be helpful, how your desire to fix might create more problems. But why do these patterns keep repeating themselves? Even with the best intentions, you can be pulled back into those reactive historical habits. This usually happens when we get emotionally triggered. Understanding our triggers is the next step to becoming the parent your kid needs you to be.

CHAPTER 10

What About Our Triggers?

"Why are you wearing makeup?" Ari's father presses, staring at his teenage son who's experimenting with eyeliner and lip gloss.

"And girls' clothes," Ari's mom adds, gesturing at the fitted jeans and flowing top.

Ari—who was assigned male at birth but is beginning to explore a female identity—sees and feels the worry, concern, and anxiety radiating from their mother's face, and the confusion and judgment coming from their father.

"I'm fine. Nothing's going on."

Ari's mother looks nervously toward her husband, adding another layer of tension to the suddenly quiet kitchen.

> Clearly, everything is not "fine," but it doesn't mean things are bad. This could have been a great opportunity for these parents to first become aware of their unconscious judgment and anxiety, set it aside, and then inquire with genuine curiosity and care about what's actually going on with their kid. Let's understand what's really happening beneath the surface of this interaction so more moments like this aren't tarnished with unconscious reactions.

THE MISSED OPPORTUNITY

Ari is starting to feel liberated and empowered by this new self-awareness of their gender identity. They're taking courageous steps toward expressing who they truly feel they are inside. But they have zero intention of sharing any of this profound personal discovery with parents whose immediate reaction is judgment and interrogation. Ari is beginning to understand they might be transgender. Despite being born male, they *feel* female. This is scary and beautiful and confusing all at once for them. It's deeply personal. But instead of curiosity or support, Ari is met with "Why are you wearing…?" as if the young person's authentic self-expression is a problem to be solved rather than a person to be understood.

What happened in that kitchen is a perfect example of how emotional triggers can hijack our best intentions. These parents love their kid deeply, but in that moment, their fear and discomfort eclipsed their capacity for curiosity and compassion. Their triggers—about gender norms, safety concerns, social acceptance—created a response that was exactly the opposite of what their child needed.

Now here's the thing: We all have moments like this. Moments when our emotional reactions sabotage the very connection we're wanting to create. The question isn't whether you'll get triggered—you will. The question is what you'll do with those triggers when they arise.

YOUR TRIGGERS ARE ROADMAPS TO FREEDOM

Listen, being emotionally triggered sucks. You feel like you're at your worst and can't seem to find a way out, even if you want to. You don't like how you feel, and you usually don't like how you act (at least not upon reflection afterward).

But when you look at the anatomy of those triggered moments, they reveal the most important ways you sabotage yourself. Triggers show you how you create barriers in your relationships and, unfortunately, how you affect your kids in ways that are completely opposite to what you intend. Yes, they always have their origins in keeping us safe, but for most of us, those uncomfortable moments of defensiveness, frustration, or withdrawal have limitations that have far outlived their original purpose.

When you become familiar with what's getting emotionally triggered inside you—not the circumstance, not the other person, not the systemic issue—you'll find a key to unlocking your own freedom.

You'll become aware of the obstacles you've created that limit your ability to live fully. These obstacles make your relationships, career, health, and especially your bond with your kids more challenging. When you reflect on why you're getting upset, you get the opportunity to see how your kids reveal an unspoken blind spot in your evolution. But what happens when parents don't do this reflective work?

LIVING IN HISTORICAL WOUNDS

Those parents who don't take time to reflect navigate feeling triggered by attempting to control how other people feel and act. They stop being strategic or curious and become reactive and impulsive because they're being driven by an internal, historical wound misplaced from another time, another situation, and usually another person.

They aren't present with their kid in front of them or the real-time situation occurring. They're stressed, anxious, upset, angry, frustrated, worried—and all of these feelings become a lens through which they see and experience their wonderful kid.

When they show up in these unintentionally reactive ways over long periods of time, their kids may start making life choices based on navigating the parent's emotional difficulties.

THE IDENTITY EXAMPLE

Let's take our example of Ari, who is exploring their gender identity. They don't tell their parents about their inner discoveries because of their parents' obvious triggers about the trans and queer community. Why would this kid unveil something so deeply meaningful about who they are, something that is currently under construction, to parents who clearly aren't curious or open-minded? Ari's parents could take away their phone, refuse to allow them to see "inappropriate" friends, and who knows what else.

WHEN TRIGGERS PUSH KIDS AWAY

The parents' emotional triggers, which they've never reflected on, communicate louder and more clearly than any conversation could. So kids who are exploring who they really are find friends who unconditionally accept and appreciate their nonconforming ideas. Unfortunately, their friends often don't have the ability to appropriately guide their fellow youth through potentially challenging explorations like this.

Ari's parents have unintentionally repelled their beloved child into the social jungle. Out there, Ari is far more willing to abandon the wonderful core family values they actually believe in just to get the connection they could have had with their parents. Ari's mom and dad unknowingly sacrificed their influence in order to keep their judgments. This pattern plays out in countless families, but it doesn't have to be this way.

DEAL WITH YOUR STUFF

The takeaway? Become aware of and then deal with your stuff. Please. Then practice extracting yourself from it.

How do you do this? Find community: therapy, coaching, personal and spiritual development seminars, and other helpful, insight- and growth-based support systems. The two most critical aspects of these support networks? Feeling supported and being challenged. Not just one or the other. Both must exist.

Find someone, or a group of people, who can supply you with equal amounts of compassion and a near-intolerance for your living in your own smallness, victimhood, or limitation. For myself, two core principles emerge whenever I am an attendee or a leader of transformational workshops: *I was loved when I thought I didn't deserve to be, and I was compassionately confronted on something I thought I didn't want to see.*

Finding the right people who can both support you when you're stuck and challenge you when you have a blind spot is critical to transformation. Why? These people can give you what so many of us never received—unshakeable care combined with appropriate, attuned boundaries. These kinds of communities can provide a living example of something we didn't have the ability to do for ourselves, let alone for others. And here's a beautiful truth that can benefit you when you engage in this work: Your external world becomes your internal world. The more you surround yourself with people and communities you want to be like, the more you become like them. The more your results look like theirs. Your relationships will get better, your circumstances will improve—your life will get leveled up.

And yet even with the best support system in the world, you'll still get triggered. The goal is to change how you relate to triggers—not to get rid of them. So let's talk about how you do that in the moment when you're overwhelmed.

ACCEPTANCE DEACTIVATES TRIGGERS

Over the twenty years I've been both practicing and teaching transformation to people, the one practice I've found to have the most surprising effect of making people feel remarkably better is *acceptance*. Acceptance of what? When we practice accepting a feeling we don't like, it dissolves. **Our acceptance of triggers dissolves them.**

If you accept you're having an unpleasant experience and face it for what it actually is—a feeling in a moment—the trigger suddenly changes from being immovable and rigid to something malleable and navigable. It might make the experience more emotional, but that's good. That means it's moving. Through acceptance of our emotional experience, we give it the permission to pass through us so that something new can be created. With consistent dedication to accepting the unpleasant emotional experience inside of us, it will dissolve over time. It has to.

Why? Acceptance is the lack of resistance. Eliminate resistance, and you have acceptance. Acceptance means you activate your heart and open yourself so the energy of life can flow. *E-motion* means energy in motion.

When you fully accept any emotion inside you, something powerful happens. You remove the internal obstacles to feeling it. Resistance, defensiveness, blame, victimhood, unworthiness—all of these come and go, and you allow the original emotion to pass.

For example, you're irritated with your spouse because they are always late. But you don't want to be irritated, because you have an important work meeting with clients where you need to be on your game and delightful. Instead of stuffing away your irritation, you take a deep breath, relax, and realize you'll have to have a(nother) conversation with them about the importance of being on time (which has you feel irritated again). Then you take another breath, accept the experience of the irritation, allow it to pass, and go to your meeting. Something is different, you realize. You're more...spacious.

This isn't compartmentalization. This isn't avoidance. This isn't even moving on. It's allowing the experience you're actually having to move *through* you. Because when it comes to emotional experiences, what we resist persists. As we allow it to move, it does—as long as we don't hold onto it or bring it back with an emotional charge like resentment or righteousness. This whole process sounds simple—and it is. But it isn't easy, at least not in the beginning.

THE THREE-STEP PROCESS

When you're really connected with whatever difficult emotional experience exists inside of you, it won't last long. It may mean you cry, let yourself be pissed, or finally feel the depth of your own despair, but eventually, with the right support and right attention, it will run its course. Once even a hint of relief occurs, take some kind of productive action. This will reinforce the space the relief is making inside your system. Go for a walk, talk to a friend, have a hard conversation where you take ownership, express vulnerability, hold a boundary, give feedback, or maybe take a bold step toward something that will move your life forward.

Here are the steps: **awareness**, **acceptance**, and **action**. Become aware of what's happening inside: *I can't believe my kid skipped school again after we had what I thought was a real heart-to-heart last night. I can't believe this is happening. I'm so f'ing pissed right now, and actually quite heartbroken. I really believed he meant every word he said. If he is high when I get home, I am going to lose my shit.*

Then practice acceptance: *I am just going to take some deep breaths. Oh my god, I can't believe he did that! What the F is wrong with him? Oops—right—I'm breathing and welcoming and accepting this anger inside me.*

Welcome the feelings of anger, resentment, fury, disappointment, and heartbreak. *Oof, heartbreak is a big one. I can't believe he would do this.* Tears start to run down your cheeks. And you just keep breathing in your heart. A tenderness comes over you because you're letting all of this just happen.

Then you take an action from the more open place inside you: You text him. *I just got a call from the school. I'm really upset with you. I'll see you tonight at 7:00 p.m.*

He texts back right away: *it's nbd mom. the school jus made a* mistake i promise i might not be home for dinner the boys are going out after practice luv u.

You take another deep breath, become aware of the flood of all those feelings coming right back again, and respond: *I'll see you at 7:00 p.m. This isn't optional.*

You're still upset—but it's more manageable now, and you're definitely more aware. The practice gave you some space to put together at least a few rational thoughts. You feel good about your clarity, your boundary, and are pensive about how you'll handle tonight. You're surprisingly relaxed because you remember he's the one responsible for his choices—not you. The school will reprimand him; you'll probably take away his phone and not let him go out for a while. But at the same time, you're actually curious about what he's going to say, despite having your doubts about this being "nbd" and just a "mistake" on the school's part. You practice these steps—awareness, acceptance, and action—a few more times throughout the afternoon and get into the routine of making dinner as you await your son's arrival. *Huh, this actually works,* you think.

The more you use this practice, the less power emotional triggers will have over you. You'll be able to parent from conscious choice rather than unconscious reaction. You'll be able to respond as the parent your kid needs instead of letting your triggers do the parenting.

Understanding your triggers also reveals something crucial about how you approach parenting itself. Triggers inspire people to lock down under tension and stress. They create compelling reasons to control rather than remain open, seek to understand through curiosity, and lean into trusting with verification when appropriate. In the previous example, the parent unsurprisingly discovers the school hadn't made a mistake; her son did, in fact, skip class. However, he sincerely owns that he lied, he really "f'ed up," and he knows he shouldn't be allowed to go out. He's seeing the severity of having so many unexcused absences at school and is realizing he's not on a good path. You're surprisingly relieved that there wasn't a huge blowup, and you can't help but wonder if your own inner work helped create this outcome (it did). Because you didn't allow yourself to get so worked up before the conversation, you actually have a delightful night of popcorn and a movie with your sweet (sometimes exasperating) son.

And even though you're still a bit upset that he broke his word from the night before, you're getting that this is his mess to clean up, not yours. Plus, something seems to have clicked for him after the talk last night and the guilt he felt from hurting you today—which is good, actually. It seems like it could be a turning point for him. And all of this was made possible because you became emotionally available to connect with him. How? You softened, so he softened. You didn't react, so he was thoughtful in his response. Your vulnerability and openness compelled him to offer the same. Your open communication about how you felt hurt and betrayed, combined with letting him know you expect him to keep his word to you, woke something up in him. That something was his heart, his goodness, and his remembrance of who he is and who he wants to be. Well done.

THE FOUNDATION BENEATH THE PRACTICE

This example shows what becomes possible when you practice the three-step process consistently. Your emotional work created space for your son's transformation. Your acceptance of your own feelings made it possible for him to accept his own responsibility.

But remember, this process only works when it's built on a foundation that many people resist—one that might challenge everything you've been taught about emotions, responsibility, and what it means to be a good parent.

This foundation is both the most difficult truth to accept in this entire book and the most liberating. It's the key that unlocks every other practice we've discussed. Without it, the three-step process becomes just another technique. With it, everything shifts.

So let's go there.

TAKE RESPONSIBILITY—NO MATTER WHAT

The outside world has an endless supply of triggers, and we think "the world" is responsible for why we feel the way we do. But the key that can completely shift every relationship in your life is this: **You—and only you—are responsible for how you feel.** You are also responsible for the meaning that creates those feelings. Most people talk about being upset by things happening out there in the world. Something happens and we're understandably affected: war, disasters, loved ones die, people betray us, the economy tanks.

There's nothing wrong with getting upset by these things. Most people would say it's natural to feel bad when something awful happens. The distinction most people miss, however, is that it's not the circumstances that create our emotional experience—it's how we relate to them. People think circumstances are responsible for how we feel. But they aren't. **They just provide compelling reasons for us to feel the way we do.** The choice of how to respond is really up to us.

This doesn't mean you should immediately be grateful when you find out your husband has cheated on you or when your mother dies. It means recognizing the distinction between *out there* and *in here*. You can't necessarily control what happens out there, but you do have a say over what happens *in here*.

A PERSONAL STORY OF LOSS

The text came at 11:47 p.m. on a Wednesday. "Call me when you get this. It's about Marcus."

I knew immediately. You don't get texts like that about good news.

Marcus had been a beloved client of mine for two years. We had an easy, collaborative, and jovial connection. He was a brilliant, sensitive kid from a family farm who had studied film at a prestigious art school. For months, we'd worked toward this moment: He had just moved to Brooklyn to pursue his passion of getting on movie sets. Just yesterday, we'd laughed on the phone about his rookie mistakes in the city—getting busted for jumping turnstiles to impress his friends, saying "please" and "thank you" so much that New Yorkers told him to "cut that shit out" because he "sounded like a freaking tourist."

Tomorrow, he was supposed to start working with my friend's production company. His lifelong dream was finally within reach.

LOSS TEACHES LOVE

His mother's voice was steady but hollow when I called her back. "Marcus died in his sleep. Fentanyl overdose. He relapsed Tuesday night."

I was gutted. I'd just spoken with him. We'd celebrated his

new apartment, his upcoming job, all the possibilities stretching out before him. Twenty-four hours later, he was gone.

I immediately focused on his mom and did what I could to comfort her. We cried together, shared memories and laughed, and then cried again. I told her I would do anything I could for her and the family. She thanked me, I thanked her for calling to let me know, and we talked about staying in touch over the coming days.

Then the rage came—white-hot and consuming. Why didn't this beautiful kid get to live his dream? I hated that he chose to get high the night before the biggest opportunity of his life. I hated that some dealer had sold him poison. I hated that all his intense therapeutic work, all his promise, had ended in a Brooklyn apartment where no one found him until it was too late. And I'm a monk. I'm supposed to be chill and understand there's some greater plan, right? Well, in that moment, I thought, *Fuck the greater plan*. I hated everything about this.

Suddenly, and viscerally, I was reminded again why we run from pain. Why we cut ourselves off from people who care about us, why we stop doing things that are "good" for us—because sometimes it's just too fucking much.

So, I screamed. I sobbed. I raged against the injustice of it all. And I shared it with the people I was closest to.

After some time, something shifted. The edges softened. The anger changed to sadness, the sadness melted into regret, the regret became...gratitude. Gratitude for what he brought to my life, what he taught me about being a kind person, about being someone who followed their dream, about the insidious nature of addiction. More than anything, Marcus reminded me about the preciousness of life. It didn't mean I liked what happened; it meant I stopped fighting the reality of it.

Nothing could have stopped me from feeling these various

dimensions of grief. I'd given everything I could to Marcus—my support, my guidance, and all my love. Then he was gone, taking all his potential with him.

But after the emotion ran its course, I saw the choice that remained: What meaning would I make of this experience?

I chose to let it teach me. To become more grateful for every pivotal conversation I facilitated, more open to understanding the depth of others' struggles, more aware of how attachment brings both love and inevitable loss. I chose to let this pain expand my capacity for compassion rather than contract it. I realized I got to know love more deeply after tasting its loss. Loss doesn't diminish love—it makes it precious.

This is what responsibility can look like in the face of tragedy: We don't choose what happens to us; we choose what it means. And the meaning I choose will always promote love, growth, and deeper connection—even in the midst of devastating loss. This isn't just philosophy—it's practical wisdom that applies directly to parenting.

Your relationship with your teenager works the same way. You can't control their choices, their struggles, or their pain. But you can choose how you respond to them. You can choose what meaning you make of their difficult moments. And you can choose to let your and their triggers teach you about your own capacity for love.

THE MIRROR YOUR CHILD HOLDS UP

The bottom line is this: **Your triggers aren't your enemy—they're your teachers.** Every time your child pushes your buttons, they're holding up a mirror showing you exactly what needs healing in yourself. Every moment you choose awareness over reactivity, or acceptance over resistance, you're not just transforming yourself—you're inspiring the same courage and resilience in your kids.

Remember, your kid doesn't need you to be perfect. They just need you to practice being open, to be willing to look at your own stuff, and to take responsibility for your inner world so you can show up as the parent they need you to be.

The question isn't whether you'll get triggered—you will. The question is: What will you do with those triggers when they come up?

THE SPACE BETWEEN

Let's be honest: This is hard fucking work. Facing your own wounds, understanding your triggers, taking responsibility for your inner world—it's a lot. And it's so critical because it isn't just personal growth. *It's the most practical and effective parenting strategy you could ever learn.*

When you do this inner work, you stop projecting your pain onto your kid's choices. You stop taking their struggles personally. You start responding instead of reacting. And in that space between trigger and response, healing is born.

So let's take the next step of understanding how your old patterns of control and fear can damage relationships. Let's learn new ways of relating to your kid that invite connection instead of resistance.

PART 3

Fundamentals of Structure

What happens when you're practicing your own work, you've started exploring your triggers, and your kid is still struggling? What do you do when it seems like love isn't enough, when understanding doesn't create change, and when your kid seems determined to destroy their life despite your best efforts?

Here's something that might challenge what you think about love: Freedom requires boundaries. Understanding doesn't exclude consequences. Sometimes, the most loving thing you can do is stop helping and start requiring. The very structure you might be afraid will push them away could be exactly what draws them back to themselves.

Your kid doesn't need another friend who enables their destruction—they need a parent courageous enough to love them and have limits. This isn't about becoming harsh or controlling; it's about becoming the container strong enough to hold their chaos until they find their center. Because a lot of parents miss this: Boundaries aren't the opposite of love—they're love made visible.

Some of you are thinking right now, "I've tried holding more boundaries. It just makes them more mad. How can limitations possibly create the freedom I want for my child?"

This resistance to structure runs deep in our culture—especially now. Many of us have been taught that freedom means having no limits, that love means saying yes, and that boundaries equal control. The very thing you fear will cage your kids, or make them more angry than they already are, could be the key to setting them free.

As an example, let me share with you the most radical

choice I've ever made—one that taught me a profound truth about the relationship between structure and freedom.

WHY I BECAME A MONK

In 2015, I was successful by most measures. I had a thriving therapy practice, had the freedom in my schedule to do nearly whatever I wanted, had an amazing group of friends, and was a high-performance rock climber. I even had a deep meditation practice, a strong spiritual community, and the most amazing spiritual teacher and guide I could imagine. Then it got even better: I fell in love. I felt like I was living in a rom com where the main character finally gets the girl of his dreams. We had a deep and powerful connection that was passionate, familiar, easy, and fulfilling.

During those months, the relationship continued to grow, and my life should have felt perfect. I had a great career, a bunch of passions, amazing friends, and now I had met the love of my life. But something was off, and I could only tell by what started happening around me.

My passion for work started to erode, my friendships felt less alive, and the fulfillment of my hobbies like climbing and backcountry skiing had less vitality. It didn't make sense. I loved this woman, and everything about the relationship felt great, but different aspects of my life started to dim as the relationship progressed. I was so conflicted. How could this relationship be simultaneously miraculous and destructive?

So I did what I always did when I felt this way—I got help. I went to a transformational workshop and did some deep contemplation. After a few days of intense work and lots of time reflecting on my own, a key choice revealed itself: *Stay in* the relationship and leave the spiritual path, or leave the relationship and deepen the path.

For a reason I can only see now, I could not have both. The epiphany was gut-wrenching. The final night of the workshop, I cried in the fetal position on the floor of my hotel room for hours. Both options were terrible: *End the relationship, or end my path.*

I chose to end the relationship. I knew eventually I would heal, and more importantly, so would she. The next day, I flew home and told her. It didn't go well. She was heartbroken, understandably upset, and desperate to convince me to stay. I waffled for a couple of days, and then I doubled down on what I knew was the right decision. I left her.

The next three months were the hardest I'd ever experienced. The vitality I had gained over the previous ten years of spiritual development had vanished. I felt low, empty, and vapid. I spent weeks alone meditating, doing breath work and other intense inner exploration. I decided I wouldn't date anyone for at least the next year—something I had never done. I would never hurt someone else like I had hurt her.

Through my solitude and reflection, a miraculous desire revealed itself: *I wanted to serve.* It was strange at first, because I had known I loved to be of service to people since I started working with kids and families in my early twenties. This wasn't a fresh insight. But something was different about it. Then another miracle occurred. *The desire for a romantic relationship disappeared.* I had yearned for a life partner since I was fourteen. That's twenty-five years. And just like that, it was gone—and it was strangely...liberating.

Some weeks passed. A few friends of mine had been planning on being initiated as *brahmacharis* (celibate monks) in the coming months. And a new desire sprouted: *Give myself to service.* Stepping away from someone meant I was available for everyone. Devotion replaced fear. This was what people meant by surrender, and my god, was it good.

A few months later, I shaved my head, was given robes, and chose for the rest of my life not to have sex, to eat only vegetarian food, not to use drugs or alcohol, and to make service to others the focal point of my life. And that was, and is, my path to liberation.

It's amazing to live a life that is so fulfilling, and at the same time to have so many self-imposed "limits." It's structure. And the structure doesn't limit my life force; it gives it shape and direction. It became the container, the vessel through which my gifts could be created and delivered. Because I refuse so much, I get access to even more.

This is the paradox of structure.

Your life force is boundless, but without structure, it leaks into distraction, confusion, and scatters like fragments of a shattered clay pot. Structure isn't a cage. It's the unbroken vessel that lets you carry your light. Structure doesn't limit; it reveals.

The shape of the pot holds emptiness. Breath gives rhythm to silence. Discipline gives form to freedom.

The structure you provide for your kids in the form of boundaries and rules will form the vessel to carry their light. Without it, their incredible energy, creativity, and potential spills everywhere, creating chaos and confusion instead of beauty and uniqueness.

Your kid who struggles isn't asking you to remove all their structure—they're asking you to *create* structure that serves them instead of your fears.

CHAPTER 11

Structural Leverage

It's 3:00 a.m., and Mateo quietly opens the front door to his family home, three hours later than he and his parents had agreed he would be home. They texted him around 1:00 a.m. to make sure he was okay, but his phone and location were off. These were all agreements they had previously made: Keep your phone on, keep your location on, and let us know if you won't be home at midnight. This was the first time he had not texted or called his parents about staying out later.

He closes the front door quietly, and his drowsy mother walks down the hallway to ask if he's okay. "Yeah, I'm fine. My phone ran out of battery." She stares at him for a moment, confused. "Seriously?" Then she turns around and goes to bed.

The next morning, Mateo and his parents have a clear, calm discussion about the importance of expectations. He understands and is grateful for his parents not punishing him for breaking his word. "Find a charger, communicate with us, do what you said you were going to do. It's simple. This won't happen again. Got it?" his father says.

"Yeah, I got it," Mateo replies.

The next weekend, the same thing happens. Literally, the same thing. It's 1:00 a.m., they text, and he doesn't respond. His location is off. This time, when he comes home at 3:30 a.m., all the doors are locked. He sees a Post-It note on the front door handle: "Doors are locked. Sleep well. See you at 7:00 a.m. for yard work." He knocks on a few doors, but no one answers.

Mateo tries unsuccessfully to sleep on the porch for a couple of hours. He's woken up at 7:00 a.m. by his dad, who hands him a rake and work gloves. Mateo spends the next five hours doing yard work and is exhausted and grumpy. His parents are having a lovely Sunday.

Over a late lunch, Mateo's parents share delightful banter about their friends, what the other kids are up to, and their plans for dinner.

"Aren't we going to talk about this?" Mateo interrupts.

His parents are silent. "Talk about what?" his mother replies after a moment.

"Listen," his father says, "there is nothing to talk about. Come home when you say you're going to, or text or call an hour before curfew. Don't turn off your location. It's not that complicated. If you don't do these things, you won't live here anymore. Any questions?"

They aren't upset; they're just clear.

Mateo attempts to explain why his phone died and why he turned off his location. One sentence in, his mom interrupts, "It's okay. Whatever happened, I'm sure you'll find a way to avoid it happening again. Let us know if you want to talk it through."

They get up from lunch, leaving Mateo at the table, "See you out there for another couple hours, Matty," his dad says over his shoulder.

Mateo sighs and noisily pushes his chair away from the table. The parents steal a smile at each other.

The parents aren't angry, they're not stressed, they don't lecture him about the importance of rules and keeping your word. **They show him.** And they don't take the choice he made personally.

It's the last time he is late for curfew or doesn't text, and he doesn't turn off his location again.

The more you can show your kid that your rules mean something, the more likely they will be to follow them.

Mateo's story is a powerful example of something that often gets overlooked in parenting: **Structure isn't about control—it's about clarity.** His parents didn't resort to yelling or punishment. They didn't plead, overexplain, or try to force his compliance. Instead, they calmly reinforced the boundary through action. They made the rule matter *without making it personal.*

Their approach worked not just because it was firm, but also because it was *grounded*. Mateo could feel that his parents weren't trying to dominate him—they were holding him accountable in a way that actually honored his ability to make choices and deal with consequences.

Now let's look more closely at what's actually happening when young people meet expectations. Following rules isn't just about discipline or respect—it's also about *courage*.

WHY FOLLOWING RULES TAKES COURAGE

A lot of parents don't realize following boundaries takes vulnerability. When a young person chooses to follow a structure they didn't create, they're essentially saying, *I trust that this rule was made with my well-being in mind.* That's not blind obedience—that's a leap of faith.

Think about it: Every time your kid comes home on time or checks in like you've asked, they're choosing to trust *your judgment* over *their momentary, self-centered impulses*. That takes courage—especially during a stage of life where autonomy and self-expression feel like oxygen.

Doing what you say means they sacrifice what they want. Can they still be who they want to be while following your rules? Cool. Then they'll probably follow most of them.

Remember, the goal isn't to demand obedience. That leads to power struggles and hidden resentment. Instead, the goal is to build boundaries that invite participation. Boundaries that *feel fair, make sense,* and—most importantly—*hold meaning.*

When a young person believes the rules are in service of their growth, not just your control, they're far more likely to buy in. And when they mess up, they'll be far more open to learning instead of defending.

Their resistance to rules isn't always a problem—it's often a sign of *life force*. That fire is part of their becoming. And when you meet it with connection, clarity, and intelligent structure, you help them turn that fire into something powerful and creative.

This understanding of resistance as life force reveals something crucial about how influence actually works with teenagers. When that fire meets the right kind of structure, it transforms into cooperation. But before we get into that, let's discuss the two primary ways you can create influence with your kid.

THE TWO TYPES OF INFLUENCE

The most powerful way to influence your kids is through connection. The second most powerful way is through leverage.

Parents provide two essential roles to teenagers: (1) a consistent, healthy **relationship** that's reliable and unconditionally loving; and (2) consistent, intelligent, attuned, and appropriately flexible **structure** to meet their ever-evolving needs.

These two types of leverage are **relational leverage** and **structural leverage**.

Relational leverage exists when your kids care about what you think and how they emotionally affect you—essentially, you have influence. When you share about how their actions have impacted you positively or negatively, it informs their choices. Parents who have fostered their connection with their kids through appropriately sharing their emotional experience have often created this kind of "leverage" naturally. However, sometimes their kids' struggle has become so great that their connection has weakened—as has their ability to create influence.

When kids struggle like this, their world becomes smaller and more self-absorbed because of the natural effect of suffering. **Remember: Suffering creates selfishness.**

So unfortunately, when young people struggle, they may stop thinking about you. Your connection with them may weaken, and your ability to have emotional influence will decrease. You try to connect, to be compassionate, to be curious, and to create influence through these noble venues, but sometimes, you fail.

This lack of connection leaves you with one of the only tools you have left: structural leverage.

WHEN STRUCTURE IS ALL YOU HAVE

This option comes into play when kids are making choices that compromise their own physical or emotional safety, the safety of the family, and the safety of others. For example, they come home two hours late after curfew, and you tell them they can't go out for the next week because they haven't learned the importance of keeping their word. You create uncomfortable consequences to inspire them to care more about important aspects of their lives.

Consequences are meant to inspire a young person to hold themselves to the standards you have for them. Your boundaries are meant to inspire internalization of those external standards. The external becomes the internal. The quality of your boundaries, and the way you hold them, will be the way your kids hold themselves accountable in the future. The best way to make this work is to stay emotionally connected through the process of communicating the consequences. Connection inspires everything.

FOUNDATION COMES FIRST

Connection lays the foundation for structure. To be effective in providing structure for your kid, you need to practice making the relationship with them strong enough to encompass any boundary you hold.

That's why we've spent so much time talking about your kid's struggles and your own. Struggles create fractures in the relationship. These fractures weaken your ability to hold boundaries, and they inhibit your ability to create healthy structure with your kids.

Once you've repaired those fractures and strengthened your connection, you're ready to create a structure that actually works. But before you set any boundary, there's one critical question you'll want to answer.

THE QUESTION THAT CHANGES EVERYTHING

Ask yourself: **What is my real intent behind this structure?**

Your first answers might be:

- *It's to keep them safe.*
- *I'm teaching them to make good decisions.*
- *I don't want them to make the same mistakes I made.*

These are all valid. And another one that drives a lot of parents is this: **I'm creating this rule so I can feel comfortable and not worry.**

WHY THIS MATTERS

Your kid can sense when you're holding boundaries for your own comfort versus holding boundaries to help them grow.

When you hold boundaries to manage your own anxiety and don't acknowledge it, you plant the seeds of opposition in your kid, and they lose trust in you.

When you get clear on how their behaviors trigger you, you can distinguish between your own historical reactions and what's actually appropriate for the situation your kid is in now. This awareness allows you to create boundaries that serve them, not just your need to feel better.

THE REAL PURPOSE OF BOUNDARIES

What is the desired outcome, and how will the boundary actually create this outcome? For example, you want your kid to be on time, so if they're late to school and the school enacts consequences, you support the school.

A young man recently told me his parents took away his phone because they found out he had been smoking weed. "I mean, that makes no sense! They have nothing to do with each other!"

After initially hearing him out and letting him vent a bit, I transitioned us into having a good, long conversation about independence. I shared how when people don't make healthy decisions with their independence, whoever governs that independence has the ability to limit it. In this case, it's his parents.

I helped him see how his choices get certain results based on the potential risks he takes. Smoking weed has pros (feeling better temporarily, making fun times better, being able to connect with friends easier) and cons (getting in trouble, making his mental health issues worse over time, becoming dependent on something to make boring times better).

I think the parents made a good choice by limiting his phone use, but they couldn't explain to him why they did it when he complained and questioned them. They just said, "That's it, you've lost your phone," so naturally it felt like a punishment. Why had they taken away their son's phone, though? Because they were upset. Their boundary was infused with that frustration. They didn't take a beat, manage their frustration and reactivity, and then thoughtfully think about what the appropriate action would be. They likely would have arrived at the same outcome—the consequence they chose—but the way they felt when coming up with it and the way they communicated it was fueled by their reactivity.

That same reactivity found its way of expressing itself to me in my session with the young man. I was able to diffuse it through hearing him out and helping him see that he consciously made the series of the choices that led to this outcome: When he'd smoked weed, he'd known something like this would happen if his parents found out. Near the end of the talk, he said something like, "I mean, I do actually get why they did this. It's just that they are both so *extra* all the time. It's like everything I do wrong is such a huge deal." Translation: His parents bring their anxiety, frustration, and emotional triggers into their relationship with their son. They let those triggers drive the communication of their boundaries—which, even their son agrees, are pretty sensible rules.

This young man's insight revealed something profound: The boundary itself wasn't the problem—the emotional charge behind it was. His parents made a good decision but delivered it in a way that obscured its purpose. Instead of experiencing a consequence that taught him about managing independence responsibly, he experienced punishment that confirmed his parents are "extra" and don't understand him.

So, what transforms a reactive consequence into a thoughtful one? Intent.

The intent of every boundary should be simply this: **to inspire your kid to become the person they want to be**. But they don't necessarily know who they want to be yet, so your boundaries are there to help them figure it out.

When parents create and communicate structure in an attuned way that actually addresses the needs, strengths, and weaknesses of their kid, they create an inspiring template for the child's own relationship with boundaries and themselves. The structure inspires discipline in them because they start to experience how that structure leads to good things happening in their life. They start to appreciate the importance of having discipline and thus dramatically increase their probability for living a life of success.

This process works best when the structure is designed intelligently—rigid enough to provide security, flexible enough to honor their growing autonomy.

THE ART OF FLEXIBLE STRUCTURE

Structure should be predictably rigid and reliably flexible. This means the structure is there when it needs to be and disappears when it's not.

It should be attuned to both the internal and external world of the child based on an understanding of both. Certain facets of the structure should be immutable—like an intolerance of violence and intentional harm, and a commitment to a path of life like school and work. There are also many aspects of the structure that are flexible—like certain schedules and expectations.

FREE CHOICE WITHIN STRUCTURE

To create an inspired structure is to allow free choice within it.

On school days, the kids are expected to be in the car by 8:00 a.m. for a departure at 8:05 a.m. If they aren't in the car at 8:00 a.m., they take the bus. This allows the kids to get up at 7:00 a.m. or 7:55 a.m., depending on their morning routine.

One of the kids smells bad and hasn't brushed their teeth? They have to take the bus. They miss the bus and are late for school? Their curfew is earlier on school nights.

And, you'll want to prepare for your kid testing this kind of clear, flexible structure when you implement it. One of their most common—and most exhausting—tactics will be the endless stream of questions. *Why this rule? Why now? Why can't I just...?*

Before you start explaining yourself into a corner, let's take a quick tangent into understanding what's really happening when they ask these questions. They endlessly ask why but don't actually want to know why? Don't waste your time and energy.

WHEN THEY ASK "WHY?"

Even if they say they want to know why, 99 percent of the times a young person asks that question, it means "I don't want to." Their "curiosity" is a great negotiation tactic meant to get what they want by stalling and wearing you down. And if they use that tactic over and over, it's because it's worked enough times for them to continue using it.

When you give your kid something after they've asked thirty-nine times, it teaches them they have to ask forty times to get it. You're teaching them that your "no" doesn't really mean no; it just means "keep asking until I'm too exhausted to hold the boundary."

This is why consistency matters more than perfection. Every time you cave after repeated asking, you're training them to think that your boundaries are negotiable through persistence rather than respect.

Discern whether their "why" is authentic. You'll know because they'll actually be curious to understand. Then and only then, explain—but don't waste your time, energy, or parental authority on insincere communication designed to wear you down.

Once you've established that your boundaries aren't negotiable through endless questioning, you can use structure in a much more powerful way. Instead of constantly defending your rules, you can start using them to teach something far more valuable: how to make good choices within clear limits. This is where structure transforms from something that feels restrictive into something that actually builds the independence kids crave.

BUILDING INDEPENDENCE THROUGH CHOICE

Structure should inspire them to be more independent and help them see value in discipline. One of your roles is to help them see their choices within the structure.

One of your kids wakes up at 7:50 a.m. for the 8:05 a.m. departure. They barely make time to brush their teeth. Then they spray on cologne on their way out the door. Later that night, they beg to stay out late on a school night to go to a concert. Your other kid gets up at 7:00 a.m. and casually makes it to the car early every morning, clean and ready to go—they also want to stay out late one night.

Obviously, you're more likely to let your more disciplined kid have more independence because you trust their ability to self-govern their life. So you do. You tell one yes and the other no. Your other kid gets upset and wants to know why. You might just say, "7:00 a.m. That's why. I actually want you to go to the concert, but you can barely get up on time when you get a full night's sleep. You want to do more stuff? Do harder things." They get upset? Fine. Don't trip into the pitfall of believing they want to understand when they really just want to vent. Arguing to attempt to get your way is not understanding.

WHEN THEY ARGUE

Remember, arguing is a negotiation tactic meant to wear you down and buy some time so they can eventually get what they want. If they are committed to a real conversation about it, do these three things:

1. **Really listen** and do your best to understand the impact of them not getting what they want. You'll have to really get it if you want them to feel understood. Empathy is power.
2. **Take ownership for being partially responsible** for their disappointment. *Yep, I said you couldn't go.* Your rules created an uncomfortable emotional situation for them. Their successful navigation of it will allow them to create a healthy relationship with discipline. You're the reason they have this "opportunity"—so just own it.
3. **Give full acknowledgment** that your choices as a parent have more power than their choices as a young person—and that can suck for them. They feel controlled or imprisoned by the choices you are making for them. *I hear you, I really*

do. I'm glad you're telling me this. And what you can remember for yourself, and tell them sometime—not now—is that how they feel about any situation is ultimately *completely* up to them. Remember, your *living* of this belief will teach them this far more than any conversation.

Don't remind them (now) that their prior choices led to your decision. That can be a "later" conversation when the iron isn't as hot. And don't explain *why* in an attempt to relieve your own anxiety for "creating their pain"—that's their pain; they created it through their choices. **They need to feel the loss of this moment in order to inspire them to show up in a more responsible way going forward.**

THE BOTTOM LINE

Structure isn't about control—it's about care made visible. When you create boundaries that serve your kid's growth instead of your own anxiety, something beautiful happens: They stop fighting the structure and start using it to build the life they actually want.

Remember Mateo's parents. They weren't angry, weren't stressed, and didn't lecture about the importance of rules. They simply showed him that their words meant something. They held the boundary with calm consistency, and it worked because the structure served him, not their need to feel better.

Structure is powerful when:

- it's rooted in connection, not control,
- it allows free choice within clear limits,
- it inspires independence, and
- it teaches kids to hold themselves to high standards.

The goal isn't compliance. It's internalization. You want them to eventually hold themselves to the same standards you have for them because they've experienced how structure creates freedom, how discipline creates possibility, and how boundaries help them grow.

Your kid doesn't need you to be perfect. They need you to be consistent. They need you to mean what you say. They need you to hold boundaries that serve their highest good, even when it's uncomfortable for both of you.

The structure you provide today becomes the self-discipline they carry tomorrow. The way you hold boundaries with them becomes the way they hold boundaries with themselves. The respect you show for your own word becomes their relationship with integrity.

Structure isn't a cage. It's the container that lets them carry their light.

Mateo's story reveals the power of consistent boundaries held without emotional charge. And knowing *when* to hold firm is just the first half of the equation. The other half is knowing *how* to communicate those boundaries—especially when your kid pushes back, argues, or tries to negotiate their way around your "no."

CHAPTER 12

Saying Yes and No

"Dad, can I get my nose pierced? Tess's mom is taking us to the piercing place after school."

"Hey, sweetie. Good morning. Nope."

"What?! Why not? It's just a tiny stud, and everyone has them now!"

"We've talked about this. It's because you're thirteen, and for us that's too young. I know this is tough for you, and I bet you're feeling left out. Plus, you probably feel like we're 'super strict' people who don't let you do anything other parents always let their kids do."

"Um yeah, that's all true, but I think you're doing it just because you like having control of me because that means you can keep me safe and I won't ever get hurt! Well, it won't work, because guess what? I get hurt every day. And having a *little, tiny* nose ring is just a little thing you could let me do so I could feel just a *little* bit better about all the terrible things I have to deal with every day!"

"Wow, you are so right. I'm sorry you experience so many awful things every day. I don't think I understood that before. Thank you for telling me."

"Yeah, I know I'm right. And yeah, it's been like this for a while now, and you've just been making it worse. So that's why getting the nose ring would help."

"Okay, I can't get too deep into this right now because I have to get on an important work call, but (1) you're absolutely right about me wanting to keep you safe, and (2) you're right about me not wanting you to ever get hurt. I *know* you're going to get hurt. You're going to grow from feeling that hurt, too, and we're still not letting you get a nose piercing. I know it's hard, and I actually appreciate hearing more about your world."

"You always do this! You make me look like a baby in front of my friends. Tess is going to think I'm such a loser!"

"I'm sorry this is disappointing for you. I know it matters a lot to you."

"Then why won't you just say yes?!"

"Because I'm your dad, and sometimes being your dad means I'm going to disappoint you."

She crosses her arms and glares.

"This is stupid. I'm going to ask Mom."

"You can ask her, but she and I have already talked about this. The answer will be the same."

"I hate you both!"

She stomps upstairs. Then an hour later, she comes back down.

"Dad?"

"Yeah?"

"If I wait until I'm fifteen, will you let me then?"

"I will absolutely consider it when you're fifteen."

"And you won't just automatically say no?"

"I won't automatically say no."

She stares longingly out the window as she stands halfway down the stairs.

"Okay. But I'm still mad about today."

"I completely understand why you would be. Want to help me with dinner?"

"I guess."

Saying no is an expression of love. Don't let this word's reputation, or your own personal history with it, convince you it's anything else.

But when your "no" comes from a place of anger, resentment, spite, or reaction, your kid's experience of the boundary shifts dramatically. Instead of "I know this is awful for you, but trust me, it's for the best and it won't last forever," your "no" means "I'm doing this to punish you, I'm doing this because I have ultimate power over you, I'm doing this because it feels good to have power over you."

Saying "no, not for now" is the best way to express a boundary that's finite in time. Remember, the primary two points of structure are to (1) keep your kids physically and emotionally safe, and (2) inspire them to create structure for themselves in their lives.

However you speak to them about boundaries is how they will speak to themselves about boundaries.

THE VOICE THEY CARRY

If you yell at your kid in anger when holding boundaries, they will do two things:

First, they'll learn to hate structure and rules, spending the better part of their young life bucking authority even if it means sacrificing their quality of life to "get back" at you.

Second, they'll internalize that angry voice. They'll leave childhood with that harsh voice inside them, affecting how they treat themselves, their world, and likely their own kids.

But this doesn't mean you should avoid saying no—quite the

opposite. Understanding the impact of how you say no should inspire you to say it more thoughtfully, not less frequently.

NO IS AN OPPORTUNITY, NOT AN OBSTACLE

Saying no isn't an obstacle to connection—it's an opportunity. Saying no creates tension, potential conflict, a heated moment. How you handle that moment reveals how much inner work you've done.

When parents handle this heat with archaic defensiveness passed down through generations, the opportunity to inspire and connect is lost. Parents who react and break emotional connection while holding boundaries lose their kids' trust almost as much as parents who don't hold any boundaries at all.

THE GASLIGHTING TRAP

Not holding any structure with a child is irresponsible and selfish. But holding boundaries without reflecting on how hard it is for them is gaslighting.

Here's why: Parents' unconscious, anxious, fear-based response fuels their kids' discontent. The kids feel their parents' anxiety and fear, bristle in response, and get understandably upset. Then parents make the conversations all about their kids' anger, frustration, and rebellion. They don't acknowledge that they were one of the origin points of the whole conflict.

These parents neglect their role in emotionally instigating their kids' disrupted response and somehow believe their child's reaction is created purely through the "neutral" communication of the rules. Without owning how they contribute to the difficulty, the child absorbs all the responsibility and then becomes doubly irritated and defiant.

This unintended gaslighting is one of the core seeds of "oppositional defiance" in young people.

Understanding this pattern raises an uncomfortable but essential question: If parents are unconsciously contributing to the very resistance they're trying to eliminate, what's driving this unconscious behavior? The answer usually lies in examining their own fears and unmet needs that get triggered when their boundaries aren't welcomed with gratitude and compliance.

WHAT ARE YOU REALLY AFRAID OF?

Let's reflect on the meaning you create when a boundary isn't received well. Are you afraid your kid won't like you or love you? Are you afraid they'll feel controlled or get angry? Do you think they aren't resilient enough to navigate this boundary? Do you not want your kid to feel like you did with your overly controlling or emotionally distant parents?

Most of the time, these fears have to do with your own insecurities about yourself. As parents, you need to be both powerful and tender, reliable and dynamic, driven and flexible, serious and playful.

Here's what this balance looks like in practice—when a parent faces their own fears about disappointing their child while still holding a necessary boundary.

A REAL-WORLD EXAMPLE

A father is letting his son know he can't go to the football game where all his friends are going because he hasn't finished homework for the class he failed the last test in.

"I told you, Elijah, you can't go out tonight. If you had done your homework earlier or yesterday, I would have been open to the idea—but you didn't, which is fine. It just means you can't go out."

"But why? I told you I'll get up early tomorrow morning and do it. Why do you always do this to me? It's like you don't want me to have friends."

Don't get pulled into his exaggerated claim about you not wanting him to have friends or how you "always" do this. Many parents engage in these passive barbs and lose their ability to communicate their larger point. Stick to the intent: **Communicate the boundary and engage in the relationship within the boundary.**

"I'm not okay with you saying you're going to do it in the morning because you've said that many times before..."

"MANY? I said I would do that once and then didn't because I was sick! Ughhhh!"

"Okay, maybe not many, but definitely more than once, and you're right about being sick that one time. Anyway, the point is you didn't get it done when you said you would, regardless of the reasons—more than the one time you were sick—so I'm not okay with you going tonight. Plus, I want you to learn to do hard things in order to get what you want. This is a key aspect of discipline, and I think if you just applied yourself..."

Elija's eyes roll so far back in his head they almost come back around from the bottom.

"Okay, okay, I won't lecture you again about discipline, but you can't go out. You need to stay in and do your homework."

"Sometimes you really suck at parenting dad, no matter how many books you read. You think that by keeping me from my friends, you'll make me actually want to do homework? Now I'm too depressed to do anything, especially homework. I hope you're happy."

"I hear you, E. I'm sorry you feel that way. Let me know if I can help you with the homework or if there's anything—"

Elijah storms away into his room.

"—you need to help you feel better. Love you."

"Whatever!" Elijah yells as he slams his door.

Parenting is about doing the best you can with what you know, faced with situations you can't control. So you show up the best you can with an open heart and a clear mind. Sometimes it hurts, and you just do the best you can to stay connected to your heart and clear in your mind—the same thing you want for your kids when they hurt.

HOW YOU SAY *NO* MATTERS

The way you communicate your "no" forms the foundation of your kid's relationship with discipline. If you're angry, frustrated, irritated, and short when you communicate boundaries, kids will avoid saying no to themselves in their own lives.

Their relationship to being told no will create such discomfort that they'll bristle anytime anyone with authority tells them no—including themselves. They'll run from authority instead of embracing the important benefits it brings: routine, structure, resilience, goal achievement, organization.

You can't control how your no will be received, but you can control the way you offer it. This sets up the opportunity for the boundary to be received, understood, and potentially followed.

Remember: Following boundaries is an act of vulnerability rooted in trust. Don't squander the opportunity for creating a trusting, vulnerable relationship with your kid on your selfish desires to be right, angry, or controlling.

This principle—saying no with love instead of frustration—applies not only to parenting, but also to how you treat yourself. When you learn to say no to yourself with the same compassion you want to show your teen, you become the kind of person worth following.

THE POWER OF REFUSING

Here's an example of how the power of *no* can transform your relationship with yourself, and thus free you up to be more effective with your kids.

A friend of mine was about to teach a weekend course with me on transformation to 150 people, and she was really struggling. It was a week before the event, and even though she knew the material well and had led courses like this many times before, she was stuck in a cycle of self-criticizing anxiety that limited her ability to be the inspiring, powerful person she was.

As the first night approached, I realized something had shifted for her. She was confident, open, and ready. I asked her what had happened.

"I refused."

"Amazing! What do you mean?"

"I refused to keep feeding that part of myself that made me doubt myself. I realized I'd had enough of that bullshit, and I decided to quit treating myself like that."

"Fantastic. What can I do to help you with this?"

"Relate to me as someone who is confident, resilient, knows

their own power and clarity, and refuses to let their critical nature rule their life."

"Boom, done."

Refusing aspects of ourselves creates space for the things we want to grow. The most productive gardens are the ones that have been carefully weeded.

This understanding reveals a profound truth about the nature of refusal itself—that every authentic *no* creates space for an even more meaningful *yes*.

NO CREATES YES

How many "no's" from others have actually led you to achieving goals you've set? How many times have you said no to yourself, and pushed yourself to continue, when you wanted to back out of a commitment?

Refusing to settle for a mediocre romantic relationship has led to meeting the partner you've always wanted. Refusing to eat poorly and avoid exercise leads to a more vibrant physical and emotional life. **Saying no wins.**

Additionally, **if you can't say no fully, your yes loses its meaning**. You run the risk of becoming fake because you are betraying yourself on a core level. You say yes in so many instances when you actually wanted to say no. You accept circumstances and decisions you could have refused. Not saying how you feel or what you really mean results in depression, anxiety, and—worst of all—an inauthentic life filled with unsatisfying relationships and a lack of fulfillment and success.

You can't say yes until you can say no.

No is the blessing of the yes. It's a necessary part of existence. For life to thrive, definition of purpose is needed.

Definitions exist only within boundaries, and boundaries come from sometimes saying no as an expression of love.

Understanding how to say yes and no with love is crucial, but it raises an even deeper question: How do you know which boundaries to set in the first place? When is structure serving their growth, and when is it serving your fear? The art of effective boundaries lies in understanding this difference.

Every parent faces moments when they question their choices—standing in hallways wondering if they're being loving or controlling, thoughtful or overprotective. These moments reveal the challenge at the heart of conscious parenting: **how to create structure that serves your teenager's development rather than just your own peace of mind.**

CHAPTER 13

The Art of Setting Boundaries

Maya slams her bedroom door so hard the picture frames rattle on the hallway wall.

"I HATE YOU! You never let me do ANYTHING!"

Her mom, Lisa, stands in the hallway feeling like she's been punched in the gut. All she did was say no to a sleepover at a friend's house where she knows there won't be any adults home.

Maybe I'm being too strict, Lisa thinks. *Maybe I should just let her go. All her friends' parents are okay with it.*

Reconsidering, her hand hovers over Maya's doorknob for a prolonged moment.

> This is the third time this week Maya has exploded when told no. Last month, Lisa gave in after a similar meltdown about going to a party. Maya came home at 2:00 a.m. smelling like alcohol, and Lisa spent the whole night terrified something had happened to her.
>
> Lisa slowly lowers her hand. She can hear Maya crying on the other side of the door.
>
> *Am I being a good mom right now? Or am I just being mean?*

"I GIVE UP. YOU'RE NOT WORTH IT."

Parents who step away from their duty of holding consistent and informed boundaries unintentionally communicate this exact message: *I give up. You're not worth it.*

The young person's defiance is their subconscious rebuttal: *Screw you. Yes, I am! Let me show you how much I don't need structure in my life!*

The parent who doesn't hold enough boundaries shirks their responsibility as a caregiver when they step away from the training and education that holding informed boundaries provides.

When you find the right boundary for the right situation and practice it consistently over time, you promote the opportunity for a remarkable life for your kid.

But how do you know if you've found the right boundary? What separates effective structure from arbitrary rules that breed resentment?

WHAT MAKES A BOUNDARY EFFECTIVE

For a boundary to be effective in the mind and world of the young person, it must be **informed**. The boundary takes into account all the necessary information needed for it to work.

This includes:

- the young person's ability to make healthy, mature decisions;
- their emotional resilience;
- their ability to learn and adapt in a dynamic environment;
- your own awareness of their abilities;
- your ability to make decisions under pressure;
- your own trust issues; and
- the nature of your relationship with your child.

One thing I've learned over all these years is that young people don't actually mind rules and structure—they mind where those things come from. When structure is born from fear, control, and reactivity, those rules forever carry those qualities. When boundaries come from care, wisdom, and thoughtfulness, kids can tell. They may still push back, but they're not fighting the boundary itself—they're testing whether you really mean it and whether it really serves them.

It's helpful to regularly reevaluate the "why" behind your boundary habits. Are they created and implemented out of fear rooted in your personal, historical reality? Are they created out of a desire to be liked, or a fear of how your kid will react? Or are they created out of misplaced frustration or reactivity born from some other aspect of your life?

Reflection is key to informed decisions, and boundary creation is no exception. This reflection becomes especially crucial when you realize that boundaries can miss the mark in two dangerous directions.

WHEN BOUNDARIES ARE TOO TIGHT

Boundaries that are too narrow suffocate. The plant grows only as much as the pot allows it. Parents who keep their kids from experiencing what the world has to offer—from the great to the uncomfortable—stop their kids from building emotional resilience.

One of the primary missions teenagers have is to experience victories and failures far from the emotional confines of the family home. They should learn to love, be hurt, heal, and then learn to love again with more discernment. They should strive and succeed, strive and fail, procrastinate and succeed, procrastinate and fail—and everything in between.

You will never keep them "safe." One of my high-performance rock climbing buddies once told me, "I get so tired of people telling me to be safe when we're high up on the wall. It's not about safety, it's about managing risk appropriately."

This is another one of your jobs as a parent: **Teach your kids to manage risk appropriately.** They won't learn to do that if they aren't exposed to risks.

But overly restrictive boundaries don't just limit risk exposure—they create something even more concerning: kids who learn to comply without thinking, who follow rules not from the wisdom of mistakes but from the fear of the unknown.

THE PROBLEM WITH BLIND OBEDIENCE

Unexamined obedience to rules is not a virtue—it's a cold, dark cell made to feel like a life. Too often young people are praised for being rule followers, but their rule following isn't based on a critical evaluation of why they follow the rules.

Seventeen-year-old Jade has perfected the art of being exactly what everyone needs. With her parents, she's the responsible eldest daughter who never causes problems. With her teachers, she's the engaged student who stays after class to ask thoughtful questions. With her friends, she's the supportive listener who never makes things about herself. With her boyfriend, she's the easygoing girlfriend who "doesn't mind" whatever he wants to do.

But alone in her room at night, Jade feels hollow. She can't remember the last time she said what she actually thought. She agrees to plans she doesn't want, eats food she doesn't like, watches movies that bore her—all while smiling and nodding. When her therapist asked her to describe herself—but without referencing other people—Jade sat in silent contemplation for a full five minutes. She had no idea who she was underneath all that pleasing.

Her "why" for following every rule, for being so agreeable, for never causing friction is a fear that if people saw who she really was—her disagreement, her opinions, her needs—they'd leave. On a core level, she feels completely unworthy of love. By pleasing others, she thinks she'll feel valuable and thereby worthy of receiving people's care. At the same time, however, she is constantly betraying herself. Her genuine desires and feelings don't even get a chance to exist. It's not like she would actually stop caring about school, misbehave, or become a terrible friend. It's just that she doesn't give her authentic feelings a moment to be experienced. She shuts them down before they can fully form.

Kids' pleasing is used to get the love from others that they don't feel for themselves. So, they become something people like. Those qualities sometimes align with who they actually want to be, but often the feelings and actions are contrary to how they truly feel. **They please others in order to get the love they don't think they deserve on their own.**

If they were secure in the innate worth they knew they had, they would practice acting with courageous authenticity, vulnerability, and boldness. They would take risks and make mistakes, sometimes appropriately pushing back on authority, knowing they have value regardless of their successes, failures, or difficulties.

But not all kids respond to controlling boundaries with compliance and pleasing. Some take the opposite path, and the results can be equally destructive.

THE ANGER ALTERNATIVE

Parents who keep their kids from living a life filled with appropriate risks and opportunities are letting their own unresolved fear and anxiety dictate the rules they create. They inadvertently pass the anxiety on to their kids, or they create so much anger toward authority figures that the kids sabotage opportunities in their life as a way of getting back at their controlling parents.

Their rage and their innate sense of unworthiness drive kids to act in ways that conveniently hurt both themselves and their parents under the guise of getting back at their parents—but they're mostly hurting themselves. Unfortunately, that hurt feels good because it confirms their brutal belief that they aren't worthy of love. People seek congruence between unconscious beliefs and outer results—even if it means doing something destructive.

Excessive boundaries suffocate growth. They create either fearful compliance or explosive rebellion. But the opposite—boundaries that barely exist—create their own devastating pattern.

WHEN BOUNDARIES ARE TOO LOOSE

Boundaries that are too loose promote instability. Parents who step away from the fire of holding boundaries neglect their responsibility and allow their kid's world to be shaped by the kid's own random, fickle, and immature desires.

We see this pattern result in entitlement and victimhood rooted in a profound lack of self-esteem. The child feels like they deserve anything they want without earning it. They feel like anything bad that happens to them couldn't possibly have to do with them or their choices.

Why? The young person who has not tasted the required bitterness of boundaries does not get to enjoy the sweet flavors of inner freedom.

THE PARADOX OF FREEDOM

External boundaries mean inner freedom. Every boundary that brings up discomfort provides an opportunity to persevere in the face of adversity—the birthplace of emotional resilience.

When young people don't experience that micro-burn of a boundary, they believe they should get whatever they want, whenever they want it. This is the nature of entitlement. Beneath the sentiment of "I deserve this" is a profound lack of self-esteem. **They don't actually believe they're capable because they haven't had to test the mettle of their personhood.**

FINDING THE SWEET SPOT

So, what is the sweet spot of boundaries? The structure should be informed by three components: **your kid**, **their environment**, and **you**.

1. **Your Kid:**
    - Their decision-making ability in the face of outside influences
    - Their maturity
    - Their emotional resilience
2. **Their Environment:**
    - Their friends
    - Larger online and real-life communities
    - The broader community where you live, including social norms and cultural influences
    - Expectations from the larger community that exist outside the family
3. **And You:**
    - Choices based on their best interests—not your irrational fears and emotional triggers
    - The intent behind your boundaries—not too tight, not too loose

How do you synthesize all these factors—your kid's needs, their environment, and your own psychology—into boundaries that actually work? The answer lies in three essential criteria.

THE THREE PILLARS OF EFFECTIVE BOUNDARIES

The boundary needs to be intelligent and thoughtful to be effective. It should come from an attuned and unattached place where you have a good idea of how the boundary will both serve the young person and promote their sense of resilience.

These three pillars make up the criteria for creating healthy boundaries:

1. **The boundary is attuned** to their emotional world.
2. **You are unattached** to how they respond to the boundary.
3. **You know** that holding this boundary is an opportunity for your kid to become more independent and more emotionally resilient.

If one of these pillars is missing or substituted with fear, trepidation, or attachment to how the boundary will make your kid uncomfortable, it runs the risk of being ineffective or divisive.

Implementing structure in your kid's life creates the possibility for them to experience comfort in the uncomfortable. **This is growth.** When someone starts to enjoy the feeling of the discomfort of growth, it means they're living a path of progress—the most fulfilling way to live one's life.

DIRECTION MATTERS

Structure should be placed in the direction they need to grow. Those kids who cling too tightly to the known world of home, familiarity, and perceived safety might need a push toward more freedom and independence. Those too close to the edge of recklessness, irresponsibility, and cavalier decision-making might need more containment.

Again, these choices should be based on an observable assessment of your kid's constitution and moral compass—not on your own comfort zone.

Boundary-setting based only on what makes you comfortable is a selfish act best reserved for the confines of a life without kids. When you become a parent, you make the choice to become selfless.

This understanding reveals something crucial about boundaries themselves—they're not just tools for managing behavior. They're windows into deeper family dynamics.

BOUNDARIES REVEAL, THEY DON'T CREATE

Here's another principle about boundaries: Their form, and the way you communicate them, can become part of your kid's struggle, but it is rarely the source. Essentially, boundaries illuminate deeper dynamics that already exist: tension between parents, tension within a parent, or of course, difficulties in the life of the child. But boundaries aren't the source. When problems arise from boundaries, it reveals something psychologically hidden.

As we've discussed, boundaries have the potential to deepen connection, not sever it. If parents can see following boundaries as an act of vulnerability, they can shape which boundaries to hold and how. This shift in perspective—from seeing boundaries as rules to seeing them as a risk to trust—can change everything about how you create them.

BOUNDARIES FROM THE HEART

Boundaries that inspire originate from the heart. They come from a place that's both attuned and unattached. They are attuned to the child's needs and informed by their emotional world.

Parents who are unattached to their child's decision-making create a helpful vacuum of responsibility which, given enough time, will be filled by the child.

One of the main problems that boundaries reveal is how a parent's anxiety drives them to feel responsible for their kid's choices. On an unseen but deeply felt level, if you care more about the outcome of a situation than your kid does, they may relate to it as something that has little to do with them.

Your emotional attachment to the outcome may cause a struggling kid to just give up on their commitments because:

1. They don't really care about the outcome or the negative impact the result will have on them.
2. They don't feel like it's their responsibility—no matter how badly you wish they did.

When you fill the vacuum of accountability that's designed for your kid, you unintentionally start to care more about their life than they do. This further distances themselves from the results they get in their life. They care less and less about their life, and thus themselves, because there isn't a compelling reason to care—the last reason they had was feeling responsible. Understanding this dynamic brings us back to the fundamental truth about what boundaries are really for.

THE SIMPLE REALITY

Boundaries aren't about control—they're about love in action. When you hold informed, attuned boundaries, you're not limiting your kid's freedom; you're teaching them how to create freedom for themselves.

Too tight, and you suffocate their growth. They become either people-pleasing rule followers afraid to take risks, or defiant rebels who sabotage their own opportunities. **Too loose, and they drown in entitlement and fragility**, believing they deserve everything without earning it, too fragile to navigate the healthy challenges of life. In both cases, they secretly feel incapable and worthless.

The sweet spot? Boundaries that come from three pillars: **attunement** to their emotional world, being **unattached** to their response, and **knowing** in your bones that this boundary helps them grow stronger.

Remember, here's the paradox: External boundaries create inner freedom. The sting of a well-placed boundary builds the emotional resilience they need to thrive.

Lisa's choice in the hallway—to hold the boundary despite Maya's tears—wasn't mean. It was selfless. If she had given in, it would have made Lisa feel better, and it certainly would have made her daughter feel better. But in this case, holding the boundary was the most loving thing she could do. **Boundaries don't just protect kids from the world; they prepare them to navigate it with strength, wisdom, and self-respect.** Lisa's story and everything we've explored brings us to this moment of integration.

LOVE MADE VISIBLE

With this book, you're building a foundation for structure that serves an understanding of why kids struggle provided in Part 1, your own inner awareness explored in Part 2, and the principles of effective boundaries outlined in Part 3. You're understanding that boundaries aren't about control—they're about love made visible. And that structure should inspire growth, not stifle it.

Even the most perfectly designed boundaries fall apart without effective communication. The most loving structure in the world won't work if you can't speak in ways that invite cooperation rather than resistance, if you can't listen in ways that make sharing feel safe.

The final piece of your transformation is learning to communicate from the heart—to speak so your kid listens, and to listen so your kid shares. Because boundaries without connection are a prison. And connection without boundaries is suffocation.

True transformation happens when structure and communication work together—when your kid feels both held and heard.

PART 4

Fundamentals of Communication

> All of us want to be heard, to be acknowledged, and to have influence. And there is one thing you can do that gets you all of this—especially with your kid: *listen with your heart.* Listen for fear, for sorrow, for resentment, for cloaked joy. Look, listen, and most importantly, feel for the message your kid is sharing. To do this, you'll have to be connected to yourself—and more precisely, you'll have to be *connected to your heart.* If you want to have influence, and you want them to share, this is the one key ingredient. So let's discuss what it actually looks like.

How do you speak so your kids listen, and how do you listen so your kids speak? Most people don't communicate in ways that inspire connection. A parent's communication reflects their level of attunement. If your communication is a struggle, look at your attunement to your kid's emotional experience. Focus on understanding rather than influencing. **Remember, influence comes from understanding.**

Effective parenting involves three main components: **being curious**, **providing unconditional care**, and **executing boundaries**. Being curious means seeking to understand without judgment, agenda, or assumptions. Being unconditionally caring means leading with your heart regardless of your kid's behavior. And executing boundaries means creating structure that helps them make increasingly healthy choices.

How you communicate all of these is the package of your love—your heart's expression. Without the right clarity and emotional stability, your parenting can contribute to your kid's struggle. Poor communication can sometimes be the very origin of their struggles.

THE RESISTANCE TO GOING DEEPER

Many years ago, I reluctantly engaged in my own personal therapy because the graduate school I attended required it. Even though I was enthusiastic about my transformation, I didn't trust therapists because I had never met one who was actually inspiring. Professionally, I was great at connecting with the young people I worked with—to a certain degree. They liked me, they trusted me, and they respected me. But I would often hit a wall with how deeply they would open up with me. Similarly in my personal life, I had strong connections with people, but there was a certain depth I couldn't create in the way I wanted to. It was hard for me to be truly vulnerable, and I struggled to cry even when a part of me wanted to. I had a sense that my professional and personal limitations were connected, and I knew therapy could help.

In hindsight, I can now see I was resistant to therapy because I wasn't willing to be vulnerable in ways that were uncomfortable. I didn't know it then, but I was deeply afraid of being hurt, judged, or taken advantage of—just like I had been in my early life. This resistance mirrored what I see in most struggling parents today. They want their teens to open up and share their struggles, but they haven't connected enough with themselves—in their own vulnerability—to give their kids a compelling reason to open up in a similar way with them.

THE ROOT OF MY FEAR

Engaging in my own personal work through therapy and graduate school helped me realize that my fear and disdain of authority came from an early trauma—at the age of six, I was molested by an older boy I trusted. When I was seventeen, I remembered this event out of nowhere and reluctantly told my best friend about it. But she didn't know how to handle the information, and she told someone else I barely knew. When I found out she'd shared this tender secret with some random kid, I was crushed. I didn't talk about it again until I started my own therapy ten years later.

These experiences taught me that vulnerability was dangerous and that trusting others could lead to betrayal. Without realizing it, I had learned to speak carefully, to share selectively, to protect myself from being truly seen—just like the kids I worked with had learned from their own experiences of being hurt and wounded.

It was through therapy that I realized why I didn't really trust anyone—especially authority figures—and why it was so difficult for me to cry. Everything was connected.

THE MOUNTAIN AND THE PEOPLE

During my second year of graduate school, our cohort went on a wilderness trip in Colorado where each of us had a three-day solo experience. I really wanted to dig deep and understand myself. I wanted to confront the parts of myself I ran from. On day three of this exploration, I reached a point where I just got fed up with how much I hid from myself and other people. In the heat of my disdain, I ran to the top of a thirteen-thousand-foot nearby mountain.

It was grueling and raw and wonderful. With every step the weather turned more and more wild, clouds grew, the wind began to rip, and sparrows darted through the gaps in the gusts. The natural world both evoked and mirrored how I felt inside. As I ran closer and closer to the summit, more and more of me peeled away. After finally reaching the summit, I broke into tears. I screamed into the wind: "I'm here and I'm broken. I don't know what to do…and I'm here."

The tears reflected a new vulnerability, a new opening into myself, a new acceptance. For the first time in my life, I let myself be real, I let down my guard—without needing to be liked or approved of. A gentle rain mixed with my tears, and I felt a deep intimacy with the natural world. The storm had reflected the moment and brought a soft rain shower that nurtured my tenderness. I experienced what it felt like to be transparent, vulnerable, and authentic.

We all returned from our solo experience, and I got the opportunity to share about my mountain climb, how hard it was for me to be vulnerable, how insecure I was, and how deeply I wished to be connected to people and to myself. I expressed my mistrust for authority figures because of the violation I'd experienced when I was a kid.

I shared everything I had hidden for so long.

And I uncontrollably sobbed.

For the first time in my adult life, I was honest with people. I was open and had nothing to hide. I was uneasy, but others seemed to feel moved—some started crying along with me, and everyone shared their support and gratitude for my vulnerability.

Living authentically doesn't mean sharing your deepest wounds and secrets with everyone around you. And it doesn't necessarily mean sharing them with your kids. **Doing inner work connects you to yourself. Sharing that vulnerability with the right people unlocks your potential to be deeply present with others.** You're not hiding anything from yourself, so you'll be able to more clearly connect with your kid. They will start to feel more comfortable sharing from their own depth because you're connecting from yours. Over time, they will stop hiding, stop faking, stop pushing you away—they will start being authentic and start trusting you with how they really feel.

This is the foundation for all effective communication with your kid who struggles: **They will listen when they feel heard. And they will share when they witness your courage to be vulnerable first.**

Following my own emotional breakthrough on the mountain and with my cohort, my ability to listen to the kids I worked with increased dramatically. They opened up to me in ways that caught me off guard. My personal relationships deepened in ways I had always wished for. I felt connected to myself in ways I hadn't thought were possible. All because I had begun the work of exploring what and how I was hiding, and then bringing it into the warm light of connection.

This lesson taught me something crucial: **Vulnerability isn't just about sharing pain—it's also about creating the conditions that allow others to share theirs.** But what does this actually look like in communication with your kids?

THE BRIDGE TO TRUE CONNECTION

Here's what I've learned in the countless conversations I've had with young people since that moment almost twenty years ago: Teens aren't just listening to our words—they're reading our energy, feeling our emotions, and sensing the gap between what we say and what we actually feel. They've become experts at detecting authenticity because their trust barometer tracks which adults are being real and which ones are performing.

When we haven't done our own emotional work, when we're speaking from our unhealed places, our kids can feel it. They sense the anxiety beneath our concern, our control beneath our care, our fear beneath our guidance. And they respond not to our words, but to that hidden emotion driving them.

This is why so many well-intentioned conversations fail. Parents think they're offering support, but they're unconsciously asking their kids to manage the parents' anxiety. Parents think they're being helpful, but they're secretly trying to control outcomes that scare them. They imagine they're connecting, but they're actually protecting themselves from feeling their kids' pain.

The bridge to true connection requires something a lot of parents aren't prepared for: emotional honesty. Not the kind where you dump your problems on your kids, but the kind where you align what you feel with what you say, where you speak from a place of authenticity instead of hidden agendas.

This means examining not just what you're saying, but also the energy driving your words. You'll need to look at the emotions you think you're hiding well, because your perceptive kid can feel them. It means becoming aware of your own triggers, your own fears, your own unmet needs, so you can speak to your kid's heart instead of from your wounds.

When you engage in this work of emotional honesty—in authentic living—everything can change. Your kid can stop having to decode your real message and can actually hear what you want them to hear. They will stop defending against your hidden anxiety and start to receive your love. They will begin to trust that you can handle their truth without falling apart or trying to fix them.

This is the foundation for all meaningful communication with kids who struggle: They will listen when they feel heard, and they will share when they witness your courage to be vulnerable.

INTEGRATION

Your work is really coming together—your deepened understanding of your kid, your practice of inner healing, the structural skills you're developing, and the communication tools you're practicing. Each piece builds on the others, creating a foundation for the kind of relationship every parent dreams of with their teenager.

Let's continue to build on these tools and principles with the goal of helping you become more and more of the parent your kid needs. Remember, your kid doesn't need you to be perfect; they need you to be real—connected to yourself. They need you to show up as someone who is doing their own work, someone who can show up for someone struggling without being consumed by their struggle, someone who loves them enough to keep growing alongside them.

This is the truth I hope you're discovering on this journey: **Who you are matters more than anything you could say or do.**

Let's continue on to the final chapters of this journey and look at how you can be someone your kids want to listen to.

CHAPTER 14

How to Speak So They Listen

A father sits across from his teenage daughter at dinner. "Where do your new friends live? Are their parents nice? What are they into—do they like sports? You met them at school, right?"

His daughter reluctantly shares superficial generalities about where they live, their music, their hatred of school, and their troubled families. But with every answer she gives, she can feel the judgment beneath her father's furrowed brow and the disapproving glances from her mom across the table. Her dad is acting like he's curious, but all she sees and feels is his disdain.

The daughter abruptly ends her sharing, and a tense silence ensues. She pokes at her pasta and realizes how much she hates sharing anything with her parents. All they do is judge her.

> "I just want to understand your world so I can support you," her father pleads.
>
> But that's not what's really happening. He wants his daughter to stop hanging out with those kids.

THE HIDDEN MESSAGE BEHIND OUR WORDS

What inspires kids to listen when we speak? The answer isn't in our words; it's in the emotion driving them. Remember, e-motion—energy in motion. It fuels everything we think, feel, and do. When we become aware of what we're actually feeling, we can become highly effective in how we communicate.

I've heard parents say the "right" thing countless times, only to watch their kid have a huge defensive reaction. Because hidden beneath those perfect words was resentment, anxiety, frustration, or judgment. The kid gets blamed for being "difficult," but part of the conflict is the disconnect between what the parent feels and what they say.

This moment—this incongruence between inner feeling and outer expression—is one of the most critical yet hidden origins of teen struggles. As we've covered, this is unintentional gaslighting. When parents remain disconnected from their own emotions, they risk making their child the problem instead of recognizing their own role in their struggle.

WHEN CONCERN BECOMES CONTROL

Consider the father who hates that his daughter has started dressing in cropped tops and short skirts. She has become more insecure, anxious, and dependent on boys' attention for validation. He can see she's struggling and is desperate to help her develop confidence, resilience, and healthy boundaries.

But his desperation has turned into anxiety, and his anxiety expresses itself as control and judgment. From his perspective, he's just concerned. But his daughter experiences something entirely different. She's conflicted because she loves her dad, but she's also so angry—he's lying without admitting it. He claims to care, but his judgment and control make that care impossible to feel.

She doesn't like sharing because it only gives him more ammunition to restrict her freedom. She becomes "defiant," but she's just protecting herself from the adults who say one thing and mean another. The gaslighting of "I care" (but I'm actually freaking out and want to control you) drives young people away from the very adults who could help them. Most authority figures haven't done the depth of inner work needed to set aside their anxiety or judgments long enough to be genuinely curious.

These perceptive young people can feel the lie, even when it's unspoken. The adult's hidden agenda destroys any chance for the teen to share their internal struggles.

THE RADICAL SOLUTION: EMOTIONAL HONESTY

Here's what actually works: Share with your kid that you're scared about their choices. Be openly concerned. Make your feelings match your words.

The disconnect between what you feel and what you say—however well-intentioned—can worsen or even create struggle in your kid. When this incongruence is intense and ongoing, it can trigger mental health issues in an otherwise healthy young person.

But a crucial distinction exists here: Share your feelings without making your kid responsible for them.

Yes, their choices might trigger you, but your emotional experience belongs entirely to you. Young people can lie, self-harm, be suicidal, or make other destructive choices that impact you and everyone around them. How you respond to these circumstances is 100 percent your responsibility.

This doesn't mean becoming a detached, calloused parent. It also doesn't mean completely falling apart and expecting your kid to behave better just so you feel better. It means handling your pain in ways that help your kid heal, not in ways that burden them even more.

AVOID THE DANGEROUS FLIP

The risk of making your kid responsible for your emotions is a role reversal in which your kid feels like they need to take care of you instead of you taking care of your kid. In this dynamic, they stop being a kid and become the parent you wish you'd had.

Kids start hiding their own emotions to manage their parent's needs, which usually results in defiance or codependence—both of which are appropriate responses to feeling like they have to be the parent who takes care of you. Defiance or anger are understandable responses to needing to fulfill a contract they didn't agree to. This codependence means they've sacrificed their childhood to take care of your feelings.

So what does healthy vulnerability look like?

VULNERABILITY WITHOUT STRINGS ATTACHED

When you share your struggles as a parent in the right way, you convey something powerful: *This is hard, and I'm okay* or *This is hard, and I will be okay. I don't need you to be responsible for me.* Don't just say you're okay—show them you're okay through your tears, your struggles, and most importantly, your resilience.

This is what creates safety for kids who struggle: They are connected to adults who can be real about their emotions while taking full responsibility for their own healing. **When you speak vulnerably without expecting anything back, over time, your kid will trust you enough to listen and to share their own struggles.**

This kind of transparency without expectation is one of the keys to creating harmony in relationships. It's also the number one reason your child will start trusting you.

WHEN HEARTS ALIGN WITH WORDS

Everything changes when you align what you feel with what you say and then share it in an honest way. Your kid will stop having to try to decode what you're really saying and will start to actually hear *you*. They'll even feel you. Because you won't be hiding behind emotions you don't want to feel. They'll stop defending against your anxiety and start to receive your love.

This honesty is revolutionary, but it's only half of the communication we're going for. Speaking authentically matters, but so does listening deeply. And most parents—even those who've learned to speak authentically from their hearts—can struggle with creating the emotional safety their kid needs to share their struggles.

Learning to listen from your heart, to hear not just their words but their pain, to respond to their vulnerability with curiosity instead of concern—this is where your relationship with them deepens, and healing starts to happen.

Teenagers will share their deepest struggles only when they know they'll be understood. And most of us have never learned how to listen in a way that creates that understanding.

CHAPTER 15

How to Listen So They Speak

Kai sits across from his parents, tears streaming down his cheeks. "My friends are family to me because they accept me for who I actually am. I can tell them *anything* and they don't judge me. I wish I could say the same about you."

His dad shifts in his chair uncomfortably. His mom stiffens. "How could you consider druggies your family?!" Kai's mother blurts out, unable to contain herself. "Those kids come from broken homes and have no direction! Why would you choose them over your own family?"

Kai's answer is devastating in its simplicity: "Because they get me, and you don't."

Silence.

I look to his parents and share, "If you want the possibility of having a relationship with your son, you'll first need to listen to what he's saying."

His mom sheds a few tears and quickly reaches for the tissue box. His dad massages his brow, pauses, and then says, "Okay, we'll try."

This vignette begs the question: How do you listen in a way that actually builds connection?

THE POWER OF REAL LISTENING

The people who are the hardest to listen to don't know how to listen. The wisest speakers are the greatest listeners. Their words carry a gravity that comes from a place of deep understanding. They have cultivated their perspective through reflection, curiosity, and inner work, not just borrowed opinions.

Ironically, one of the best ways to influence a teenager is to stop talking. Don't give direction. Don't share your "life lessons." Don't try to fix them. Just be with them and listen.

EMPTY YOUR CUP FIRST

You can't be present with someone who needs you while carrying your own unresolved emotional baggage. If you're anxious, depressed, frustrated, or troubled by other aspects of your life, you're lying to your kid if you don't acknowledge that difficulty in some appropriate way with them.

Empty your cup through your own emotional work before you show up for their pain. You limit your ability to have influence when you can't listen fully. And you can't listen fully when you're secretly prioritizing your own pain over theirs.

LISTEN FROM YOUR HEART

Real listening requires a relationship with your own heart. Practice being able to soften, breathe, and accept yourself with humility. Practice acknowledging your mistakes, your selfishness, your weaknesses.

But also practice knowing your value—your strengths and gifts that help others. Being connected to your heart means not letting your inner critic define your reality. You will need to foster enough grit in you to confront that critical voice and cultivate the vitality and the resilience that inspires others.

When you listen from this place of vulnerable strength, you give your kid permission to feel their own heart. Remember, however you are, so are they. When you listen with an unselfish heart yearning to understand rather than solve, you teach them to do the same. Here's what this can look like in practice—and what happens when we get it wrong.

"You don't know me."

Kai's parents came to me furious about their son's daily cannabis use and rule-breaking. They'd tried everything—early curfews, drug tests, therapy, restrictions. Nothing worked.

It quickly became clear how little they knew about his inner world. Every time he tried to share something meaningful, they criticized his choices. He felt like he couldn't do anything right.

Now we can't say for certain this young man wouldn't have made these choices if his parents were better listeners. But there would have been a hell of a lot higher chance of Kai making better choices if his parents were dedicated to "getting him."

If his pain and frustration were welcomed with curiosity instead of reactive judgment, he might not have searched for connection so far outside his family's orbit. Teenagers always find someone to connect with. Do anything you can to make it into that coveted group.

DEPTH CREATES TRUST

Kids who struggle can smell superficiality miles away. They've been forced into their own depths through emotional challenges, so now they have the ability to know when people are talking bullshit or actually mean what they're saying. Their suffering breeds a kind of wisdom a lot of us never learned. So, the more you explore your own pain, meaning, and growth, the more you become someone who can be trusted. The more you deepen your relationship with yourself, the better equipped you become to actually understand them.

Through knowing yourself, you create the possibility of knowing them. Your inquiry leads to trust. They start trusting you and, in doing so, learn to trust themselves.

Remember, listening requires depth. Depth leads to understanding. If we really want to understand someone whose experience is different from our own, we will have to set aside our own self-absorbed opinions, ideas, and desires.

THE ASSIGNMENT

Your primary job as the parent of a kid who struggles is to create a compelling experience for them to unlock themselves from the prison cell they've retreated to. Being genuinely curious becomes a reason for them to share and thus start to heal.

Listen to them so you can discover what's driving their

choices and behaviors. If you can see how your own unconscious feelings fuel your words and actions, you'll have insight into the same process in your kid.

Look to see what drives *your* moods and what feelings drive *your* choices. Then apply that same depth of listening to your kid. Their choices are expressions of feelings and beliefs—waves informed by a unique, tender, and powerful current.

If you start understanding this depth in yourself, you'll dramatically increase your ability to understand your kids. And as we've discussed, understanding is the first step toward influence. When your kid starts to really feel understood, they'll begin to see you as someone reliable enough to share their struggles with.

LISTENING IN THE STORM

You're learning how to speak authentically and listen deeply. To empty your own cup first. You're also learning why curiosity is more powerful than advice, and why your kid will share more when they feel and witness your courage to be vulnerable.

Let's see how to apply all of this when things get really hard—when emotions are running high, and stakes feel enormous—when every word seems to matter. These moments often require more than the right intentions; they require a specific framework that can hold both your fear and your kid's pain.

The hard conversations—the ones about drugs, lying, stealing, failing grades, dangerous friends, self-harm—these don't happen in ideal conditions. They happen when you're terrified, when your kid is defensive, when trust is broken. These are the exact moments when clear and authentic communication matters most.

Here's how to navigate hard conversations with courage, compassion, and clarity.

CHAPTER 16

The Hard Conversation

The tension is palpable. Your son is in trouble at school—again. Your husband is pissed because your son is being cruel to his younger sister—again. You're torn between feeling that same frustration with everything and everyone, and knowing you can't feel this way if you're going to connect with your son and actually have a productive conversation with him.

You remember you have to get to a place of genuine curiosity, and that takes compassion and patience. So, you take a breath and ask him to come sit with you outside on the porch. It's silent and tense, and you're not really sure what to do. Then you remember the one thing you've heard is supposed to work in moments like this: You listen.

"Tell me," you say.

He shares, little by little, and you just absorb. You start to get him. You start to understand. You start learning about him. You're hearing a nuance you haven't heard before, and something is clicking in a new way. It's strange, but even though a part of you is still upset about how he's been treating the family, a growing part of you is starting to understand why. It doesn't excuse the impact he has had on people, but it does...make so much more sense now. A wave of gratitude rushes over you, and you start welling up in the middle of his narrative.

"Mom, are you okay? I'm not trying to make you mad."

"No, sweetie, I'm just so grateful you're sharing so much. Everything is just starting to make so much more sense. Thank you."

What you need to do emerges from understanding.

Let's talk about how to make this happen.

SETTING UP FOR SUCCESS

It's time for that conversation you've been avoiding and your son has been dreading. These talks haven't gone well before, but let's set this one up differently.

Find the ideal time and neutral territory—ideally somewhere he feels comfortable. No phones, no music, no distractions. Set a realistic time frame for the conversation and tell everyone the expectations in advance.

Create a quick agenda with a clear intent: "I want to talk for the next thirty minutes about what's happening for you, because the choices you're making are affecting you, me, and the family. I want to understand more so I can help. Make sense?"

"Whatever."

"Okay, so what's going on?"

Silence.

"If you're not going to share, that's okay, but then I'll just have to do my best to create some rules around your life that you probably won't like—because I won't understand. It's up to you."

"Fine. Your rules are lame, you're too strict, you don't get kids today, you think I'm just like you when you were young, and you don't actually know what I care about."

Hallelujah! This is really great information.

A lot of parents sabotage themselves in this moment because all they can hear is criticism, so they just get defensive. But not you. You're doing your own work, and you know how important it is to understand so you can actually help and not make a bigger mess than this already is.

"Wow, okay, thank you. It sounds like you don't trust my perspective on your life, so my rules feel completely off from what you actually need. Is that right?"

"Um, yeah, pretty much."

This is the beginning of what it looks like to be disarmed. You've given him a compelling reason to lower his defenses—even just a little—because you're humble enough to admit you might not know everything.

"Here's what I'd like to do. Give us some feedback on what you think we should be doing differently as your parents. We may not agree with all of it, but it doesn't matter. I really want to hear from you."

"Well, you're way stricter than everyone else, your rules don't actually help my problems, and you criticize how I dress and what music I listen to. You don't accept who I actually am."

"Okay, thank you. This is helpful. So, tell me, who are you and who do you want to be?"

He goes on a long diatribe about how the rules you set don't actually allow him to be who he wants to be. If he can't do what he wants, he can't be who he wants. He peppers in personal feedback about how you and his dad are too bossy, too controlling, too nosey, and too out of touch. His dialogue is filled with equal parts blame, self-absorbed immaturity, and gems about how his life is actually really confusing and hard. He knows he shouldn't be doing the things he's doing, but he's deeply conflicted and doesn't know how to navigate all the competing desires he has.

It's tempting to challenge him on how he doesn't take responsibility, isn't willing to see situations from any perspective but his own entitled views, and how the music he listens to is filled with derision of women and the glorification of money, cars, and jewelry. Part of you wants to make him see how bad all this is for him—but you know better, so you don't say or do that, even though some part of you would love to. So, you take a deep breath and figuratively take a large step over the blame and immaturity toward the part of his sharing that really matters: the desires he's conflicted about and the choices he's making that he knows aren't great.

"Well, first, thank you. I really appreciate hearing so much about how you experience your world and us. Seriously, I'm so glad you're opening up. I want to talk more about all of this in our family session tomorrow if you're up for it. So let's wrap up for now since we're getting close to the end of our thirty minutes. For tonight, make sure to come home before curfew and clean up the kitchen before you go. I'd rather not create stupid consequences just because you don't do the dishes or get home on time. Deal?"

"I can't promise I'll be home on time if my friends and I are having an awesome time. That's your rule, not mine."

Stay the course. Hold the gentle line without igniting conflict.

"I hear you. And if you come home past curfew without checking in, you'll lose driving privileges like we discussed. It's up to you."

"Whatever. I knew this talk wouldn't change anything. Bye."

WHAT JUST HAPPENED

This didn't end how you wanted it to, but that's okay. You met some key goals: understanding your son's life, hearing honest vulnerability, and learning his priorities. Don't get too bothered by how he flipped the middle finger at your rules.

He's selfish—and that's normal. Kids aren't incentivized to do what you want. They get more value from what they want to do than from doing what you want them to do. Time with their friends is usually their respite from everything. Your strategy is to create enough opportunities through relationships and structure to help them feel better in more ways than just from hanging out with friends.

Remember your goals: (1) get connected, (2) appreciate a different view, and (3) convey boundaries inspired by understanding. Your kid doesn't have to like the boundary—it just needs to be informed by what they shared. This example shows the structure, so now let's break down the specific techniques that make these conversations work.

THE FORMAT THAT WORKS

Start with accountability. "Things have been hard between us, and I want to say that how I've responded hasn't been the best. I've been stressed, sometimes reactive, and narrow-minded. I haven't shown up like I've always wanted to. The stress in our relationship affects me a lot, and I want to talk so we both feel better. I'm not saying it's your fault—I just care about you, and things don't feel right when we're not in a good place."

You're creating a soft, vulnerable vibe and modeling accountability. As the family leader, you set the conversation's tone. You're also demonstrating it's safe to be vulnerable here.

Make statements instead of asking questions. "Tell me about how things are going in your world." Questions generally put people in their heads and have them think about things instead of sharing feelings. They bring us into concepts instead of the heart.

Be patient with victimhood. If they blame everything on outside forces, don't confront it now. Be genuinely curious about how the world occurs to them.

"Everyone at school is a dick. I'm never going back."

"Okay, tell me about what makes them so cruel."

"Every time I'm late, the teacher glares at me and the other kids chuckle like assholes."

Resist saying "I wish you wouldn't use words like that" or "Maybe if you weren't late none of this would happen." They already know you don't like when they swear, and they know about the obvious solutions to their problems. You're building connection so they trust you and don't feel alone.

"That sounds embarrassing and really upsetting. What's your plan for handling it?"

"I'm not going back."

"I can get how awful it must be. It sounds humiliating. But... you can't just never go back to school. Let's explore other solutions."

"If you can quit a job and get a new one, I can switch schools."

"That's actually a fair point. We're not quitting this school yet, but I get how uncomfortable this is. Do you want any support navigating it?"

"No. I hate them."

"Huh. All right, well, I really want to help you, but I get it if you want to handle it yourself. I know you'll find some way to figure it all out. Let me know if there's anything I can do. Want pancakes?"

"Mom, it's ten o'clock at night, and I have school tomorrow."

"So...no?"

"Okay, but just one. You're so weird."

"Great!" You start gathering ingredients. You'd like nothing more than to go to bed, because you're actually exhausted, but you know he loves pancakes and want him to know how much you care about him. He'll feel your care if you do this—and that's important to you.

You both share some small talk about other subjects while you're cooking, and the mood turns light and jovial. You purposely don't bring up the topic of school again because you are consciously relating to it as his responsibility—not yours. He knows you won't let him quit or switch schools, so you just let him stay in the tension of his situation. The strategy here is this: **Create a warm connection inside the definition of the boundary.** *I'll make you pancakes; you'll figure out the school situation.*

This example illustrates the techniques, and there's one critical principle underlying all of this that is important to underscore.

THE RESPONSIBILITY PRINCIPLE

It's not your job to relieve their tension. When you start feeling more stressed than your kid does about their life, you become responsible for their life. Stress expresses responsibility—if you're holding the stress for their poor choices, they conveniently don't have to. That stress is what motivates people to do something different. If you relieve your kid of the stress of needing to make a new choice, you limit their ability to change and adapt.

This is one of the main pitfalls of parenting kids who struggle. Give them back the responsibility for their life and focus on caring for yourself strategically so you can help them when they actually need it.

What can make these conversations disorienting is that without the familiar endpoint of compliance or agreement or even a plan, a lot of parents aren't sure what they are actually trying to accomplish.

THE REAL GOAL

These talks are challenging because there's usually no mutual interest toward a shared goal. Make the goal understanding first, and then decide what to do second. Remember, **what to do emerges from understanding**. This strategy creates the possibility of connection, which conveniently makes it possible for the kids to actually feel better.

Your kid's struggle may not be something you can fix, but it's an opportunity for you to love more deeply, listen more intently, and—just maybe—help them feel better. When you practice this approach with courage and compassion, a profound shift becomes possible.

EVERYTHING COMES TOGETHER

Everything you've learned here increases the chance that you can help: the understanding to look beyond behavior to pain, the self-awareness to respond instead of react, the ability to create structure that serves, and the communication skills to connect even in difficult times. You're learning to speak authentically and listen from love, to navigate the hardest conversations with grace, and to create a sanctuary for vulnerability even in those tough times. Each piece builds on the others, creating that possibility for something deep and meaningful to occur.

As you're learning, communication isn't about perfect words—it's about the energy behind the words, the heart that fuels the conversation. Remember, **who you are is more important than what you say**.

Your transformation is their invitation to transform. Your healing creates space for their healing. You can only take someone as far as you've gone yourself. And while it may seem like the journey is just beginning, the step you've taken by reading this book is a huge one. You've left behind one way of being and entered another—one that is more connected to yourself and can therefore be more connected to your kids. The parent you're becoming through this journey isn't just the parent your kid needs right now. It's the parent they'll need as they continue to grow, and likely, the grandparent their children will someday need.

Who you are is how you parent.

Conclusion

> Who you are shapes who they'll become. Who you've been in your pain has contributed to who they are in their pain now. Who you're becoming in your transformation is revealing, right now, who they will become in theirs. You are becoming their invitation to heal.

THE NIGHT THAT CHANGED EVERYTHING

When I was seventeen, I thought about killing myself. One night, I took a pairing knife out of the kitchen drawer and held it next to my wrist. I stood there silently, the ticking of the clock in the background as it passed 2:35 a.m. I was tired of feeling so lonely and so worthless, of trying so hard to be someone people liked—and I was tired of not being able to articulate any of it. But something powerfully good and mysterious stopped me—something subtle and quiet, something stronger than the pain.

In hindsight, I can see there was a love inside me I hadn't yet discovered, a love that revealed itself the more I opened to it. A love whose foundation, I can now see, was created by my parents. As much as I pushed them away, as much as I thought I hated them nearly every day of my adolescence, they loved me—and they always did their best to make me feel it.

You're doing your best right now. You've spent precious moments of your life learning, growing, and practicing so you can become the kind of person, the kind of parent, that can help your kid. You're dedicated, you're willing, you're open. And your kid is feeling it. Somewhere inside, they can feel that same tug to be more open, to be more courageous, to be more connected—just like you're becoming.

I didn't kill myself that night because a silent, inner urge toward life was greater than the pain.

That same urge toward life exists in your kid—and you're fostering it with every word you read.

THE JOURNEY YOU'VE TAKEN

You've traveled far on this journey—from feeling helpless and confused to beginning to understand both your kid's struggles and your own. You've looked in mirrors that most parents never dare to face. You've started the inner work that creates real transformation.

What you've learned isn't just concepts and strategies—it's also the foundation for a new way of being with your kid and with yourself. A way rooted in understanding instead of control, in presence instead of reaction, and in love instead of fear.

Your kid needs you to become the person capable of understanding them, not fixing them. They need you to do your own inner work so you can support them in theirs. Most of all, they need you to remember that **who you are matters more than anything you could ever say or do.**

Again, you can only take someone as far as you've gone yourself. And the parent you're becoming through this inner work isn't just what your kid needs now—it's what they'll carry forward for the rest of their lives.

Become who your child needs you to be, and you'll become more of who you actually are.

Resources

For additional resources, speaking engagements, and to explore working with Jivan Das, visit:

Join Jivan Das on social media:

www.ingramcontent.com/pod-product-compliance
Lightning Source LLC
LaVergne TN
LVHW041632060526
838200LV00040B/1544